THE ARIAN CONTROVERSY

THE
ARIAN CONTROVERSY.

BY

H. M. GWATKIN, M.A.
LECTURER AND LATE FELLOW OF ST JOHN'S COLLEGE,
CAMBRIDGE

Second Edition.

WIPF & STOCK · Eugene, Oregon

Wipf and Stock Publishers
199 W 8th Ave, Suite 3
Eugene, OR 97401

The Arian Controversy, Second Edition
By Gwatkin, Henry M.
Softcover ISBN-13: 978-1-6667-3138-5
Hardcover ISBN-13: 978-1-6667-2382-3
eBook ISBN-13: 978-1-6667-2383-0
Publication date 6/16/2021
Previously published by
Longmans, Green, and Co., 1891

This edition is a scanned facsimile
of the original edition published in 1891.

CONTENTS.

	PAGE
LIST OF WORKS	IX

CHAPTER I

| THE BEGINNINGS OF ARIANISM | 1 |

CHAPTER II.

| THE COUNCIL OF NICÆA | 16 |

CHAPTER III.

| THE EUSEBIAN REACTION | 41 |

CHAPTER IV.

| THE COUNCIL OF SARDICA | 61 |

CHAPTER V.

| THE VICTORY OF ARIANISM | 80 |

CHAPTER VI.

| THE REIGN OF JULIAN | 105 |

CHAPTER VII.

THE RESTORED HOMŒAN SUPREMACY . . . 118

CHAPTER VIII

THE FALL OF ARIANISM . . 147

CHRONOLOGICAL TABLE . . . 169

INDEX 173

LIST OF WORKS.

THE following works will be found useful by students who are willing to pursue the subject further. Some of special interest or importance are marked with an asterisk.

(A.) ORIGINAL AUTHORITIES AND TRANSLATIONS.

The Church Histories of *Socrates, Sozomen, Theodoret, and (for the Arian side) the fragments of Philostorgius [translations in Bohn's *Ecclesiastical Library*].

*Eusebius, *Vita Constantini* and *Contra Marcellum Ancyranum*

*Athanasius, especially *De Incarnatione Verbi Dei*, *De Decretis Synodi Nicænæ*, *Orationes contra Arianos*, *De Synodis*, *Ad Antiochenos*, *Ad Afros*. Convenient editions of most of these by Professor Bright of Oxford. [Translations of **De Incarnatione* (Bindley in *Christian Classics* Series) and of the *Orationes* and most of the historical works, Newman in Oxford *Library of the Fathers*]

Hilary, especially *De Synodis*. Cyril's *Catecheses* [translation in *Oxford Library of the Fathers*]. Basil, especially *Letters*. Gregory of Nazianzus, especially *Orationes* iv. and v. (against Julian). Of minor writers, Phœbadius and Sulpicius Severus (for Council of Ariminum). Fragments of Marcellus, collected by Rettberg (Gottingen, 1794). [German translations of most of these in Thalhofer's *Bibliothek der Kirchenvater*. English may be hoped for in

Schaff's *Select Library of the Nicene and Post-Nicene Fathers* (vol. i. Buffalo, 1886) in 25 vols]

Heathen writers :—Zosimus (bitterly prejudiced); Ammianus Marcellinus for 353-378 (cool and impartial); Julian, especially *Cæsares, Fragmentum Epistolæ*, and *Epp.* 7, 25, 26, 42, 43, 49, 52.

(B.) MODERN WRITERS.

1. For general reference :—

Gibbon's *Decline and Fall* (prejudiced against the Christian Empire, but narrative still unrivalled); Schiller *Geschichte der romischen Kaiserzeit*, Bd. ii. (church matters a weak point); Ranke, *Weltgeschichte*, Bd. iii. iv.

General Church Histories of Neander [translation in Bohn's *Standard Library*]; Kurtz (zehnte Aufl., 1887); Fisher (New York, 1887); also Hefele, *History of the Church Councils* [translation published by T. & T. Clark].

Articles in *Dictionary of Christian Biography* (especially those by Lightfoot, Reynolds, and Wordsworth), and in Herzog's *Realencyclopadie* (especially *Monchtum* by Weingarten).

Weingarten's *Zeittafeln z. Kirchengeschichte* (3 Aufl. 1888).

(2.) For special use :—

The whole period is more or less covered by Kaye, *Some Account of the Nicene Council*, 1853, *Stanley, *Eastern Church* (best account of the outside of the council); Broglie, *L'Église et l'Empire romain ;* Gwatkin, *Studies of Arianism*, 1882.

On Constantine, Burckhardt, *Die Zeit Constantins*, 1853; Keim, *Der Uebertritt Constantins*, 1862; Brieger, *Constantin der Grosse als Religionspolitiker*, 1880.

On Julian, English account by *Rendall, 1879; German lives by Neander, 1813 [translated 1850]; Mucke, 1867-69, and Rode, 1877. The French books are mostly bad. For the decline of heathenism generally, Merivale, *Boyle Lectures* for 1864-65; Chastel, *Destruction du Paganisme*, 1850; Lasaulx, *Untergang des Hellenismus*, 1854; Schultze, *Geschichte des Untergangs des griechisch-romischen Heidentums*, 1887; also Capes, *University Life in Ancient Athens*, 1877; Sievers, *Leben des Libanius*, 1868.

Biographies:—Fialon, *Saint Athanase*, 1877 (slight, but suggestive); Zahn, *Marcellus von Ancyra*, 1867; Reinkens, *Hilarius von Poitiers*, 1864; Fialon, *Saint Basile*, 1868; Ullmann, *Gregorius von Nazianz*, 2 Aufl. 1867 [translated 1851]; Kruger, *Lucifer von Calaris*, 1886; Eichhorn, *Athanasii de vita ascetica Testimonia*, 1886 (in opposition to Weingarten and others); Guldenpenning u. Ifland, *Theodosius der Grosse*, 1878; various of unequal merit in *The Fathers for English Readers*.

On Teutonic Arianism:—Scott, *Ulfilas, Apostle of the Goths*, 1885; Hodgkin, *Italy and her Invaders*, 1880-85; Revillout, *De l'Arianisme des Peuples germaniques*, 1850.

For doctrine, the general histories in German of Baur, Nitzsch, 1870; Hagenbach [translated in Clark's *Foreign Theological Library*], and *Harnack, Bd. ii., 1887; Dorner's *Doctrine of the Person of Christ* [translated in Clark's *Foreign Theological Library*]; *Hort, *Two Dissertations*, 1876 (on Nicene and Constantinopolitan Creeds); Caspari, *Quellen*, Bd. iii. (on Apostles' Creed).

On Athanasius, also Voigt, *Die Lehre von Athanasius*, 1861; Atzberger, *Die Logoslehre des hl. Athanasius*, 1880; Wilde, *Athanasius als Bestrijder der Arianen*, 1868 (Dutch).

For the Roman Catholic version of the history, Mohler, *Athanasius der Grosse*, 1844; Newman, *Arians of the Fourth Century*.

For short sketches giving the relation of Arianism to Church history in general, *Allen, *Continuity of Christian Thought*, 1884 (contrast of Greek and Latin Churches); *Sohm, *Kirchengeschichte im Abriss*, 1888.

NOTE.

The present work is largely, though not entirely, an abridgement of my *Studies of Arianism.*

The Conversion of the Goths, which gives the best side of Arianism, has been omitted as belonging more properly to another volume of the series.

THE ARIAN CONTROVERSY.

CHAPTER I.

THE BEGINNINGS OF ARIANISM.

ARIANISM is extinct only in the sense that it has long ceased to furnish party names. It sprang from permanent tendencies of human nature, and raised questions whose interest can never perish. As long as the Agnostic and the Evolutionist are with us, the old battlefields of Athanasius will not be left to silence. Moreover, no writer more directly joins the new world of Teutonic Christianity with the old of Greek and Roman heathenism. Arianism began its career partly as a theory of Christianity, partly as an Eastern reaction of philosophy against a gospel of the Son of God. Through sixty years of ups and downs and stormy controversy it fought, and not without success, for the dominion of the world. When it was at last rejected by the Empire, it fell back upon its converts among the Northern nations, and renewed the contest as a Western reaction of Teutonic pride against a Roman gospel. The struggle went on for full three hundred years in all, and on a scale of vastness never seen again in history. Even the Reformation was limited to the West, whereas Arianism ranged at one time or another through the whole of Christendom. Nor was the battle merely for the wording of antiquated creeds or for the outworks of the faith, but for the very life of revelation. If the Reformation decided the supremacy of revelation over church authority, it was the contest with Arianism which cleared the way, by settling for ages the deeper and still more momentous question, which is once more coming to the surface as the gravest doubt of our time, whether a revelation is possible at all.

Unlike the founders of religions, Jesus of Nazareth made his own person the centre of his message.

The doctrine of the Lord's person. Through every act and utterance recorded of him there runs a clear undoubting self-assertion, utterly unknown to Moses or Mahomet. He never spoke but with authority. His first disciples told how he began his ministry by altering the word which was said to them of old time, and ended it by calmly claiming to be the future Judge of all men. And they told the story of their own life also; how they had seen his glory while he dwelt among them, and how their risen Lord had sent them forth to be his witnesses to all the nations. Whatever might be doubtful, their personal knowledge of the Lord was sure and certain, and of necessity became the base and starting-point of their teaching. In Christ all things were new. From him they learned the meaning of their ancient scriptures; through him they knew their Heavenly Father; in him they saw their Saviour from this present world, and to him

they looked for the crown of life in that to come.
His word was law, his love was life, and in his name
the world was overcome already. What mattered it
to analyse the power of life they felt within them?
It was enough to live and to rejoice; and their works
are one long hymn of triumphant hope and overflowing thankfulness.

It was easier for the first disciples to declare what
their own eyes had seen and their own hands had
handled of the Word of Life, than for
another generation to take up a record
which to themselves was only history, and
to pass from the traditional assertion of the Lord's
divinity to its deliberate enunciation in clear consciousness of the difficulties which gathered round it when
the gospel came under the keen scrutiny of thoughtful heathens. Whatever vice might be in heathenism,
there was no want of interest in religion. If the
doubts of some were real, the scoffs of many were
only surface-deep. If the old legends of Olympus
were outworn, philosophy was still a living faith, and
every sort of superstition flourished luxuriantly. Old
worships were revived, the ends of the earth were
searched for new ones. Isis or Mithras might help
where Jupiter was powerless, and uncouth lustrations
of the blood of bulls and goats might peradventure
cast a spell upon eternity. The age was too sad to
be an irreligious one. Thus from whatever quarter
a convert might approach the gospel, he brought
earlier ideas to bear upon its central question of the
person of the Lord. Who then was this man who
was dead, whom all the churches affirmed to be alive

In contact (1) with the vulgar

and worshipped as the Son of God? If he was divine, there must be two Gods; if not, his worship was no better than the vulgar worships of the dead. In either case, there seemed to be no escape from the charge of polytheism.

The key of the difficulty is on its other side, in the doctrine of the unity of God, which was not only taught by Jews and Christians, but generally admitted by serious heathens. The philosophers spoke of a dim Supreme far off from men, and even the polytheists were not unwilling to subordinate their motley crew of gods to some mysterious divinity beyond them all. So far there was a general agreement. But underneath this seeming harmony there was a deep divergence. Resting on a firm basis of historic revelation, Christianity could bear record of a God who loved the world and of a Redeemer who had come in human flesh. As this coming is enough to show that God is something more than abstract perfection and infinity, there is nothing incredible in a real incarnation, or in a real trinity inside the unity of God. But the heathen had no historic revelation of a living hope to sustain him in that age of failure and exhaustion. Nature was just as mighty, just as ruthless then as now, and the gospel was not yet the spring of hope it is in modern life. In our time the very enemies of the cross are living in its light, and drawing at their pleasure from the well of Christian hope. It was not yet so in that age. Brave men like Marcus Aurelius could only do their duty with hopeless courage, and worship as they

(2) with the philosophers.

might a God who seemed to refuse all answer to the great and bitter cry of mankind. If he cares for men, why does he let them perish? The less he has to do with us, the better we can understand our evil plight. Thus their Supreme was far beyond the weakness of human sympathy. They made him less a person than a thing or an idea, enveloped in clouds of mysticism and abolished from the world by his very exaltation over it. He must not touch it lest it perish. The Redeemer whom the Christians worship may be a hero or a prophet, an angel or a demigod—anything except a Son of God in human form. We shall have to find some explanation for the scandal of the incarnation.

Arianism is Christianity shaped by thoughts like these. Its author was no mere bustling schemer,

<small>Arius himself</small> but a grave and blameless presbyter of Alexandria. Arius was a disciple of the greatest critic of his time, the venerated martyr Lucian of Antioch. He had a name for learning, and his letters bear witness to his dialectical skill and mastery of subtle irony. At the outbreak of the controversy, about the year 318, we find him in charge of the church of Baucalis at Alexandria, and in high favour with his bishop, Alexander. It was no love of heathenism, but a real difficulty of the gospel which led him to form a new theory. His aim was not to lower the person of the Lord or to refuse him worship, but to defend that worship from the charge of polytheism. Starting from the Lord's humanity, he was ready to add to it everything short of the fullest deity. He could not get over the philosophical diffi-

culty that one who is man cannot be also God, and therefore a second God. Let us see how high a creature can be raised without making him essentially divine.

The Arian Christ is indeed a lofty creature. He claims our worship as the image of the Father, begotten before all worlds, as the Son of God, by whom all things were made, who for us men took flesh and suffered and rose again, and sat down at the right hand of the Father, and remains both King and God for ever. Is not this a good confession? What more can we want? Why should all this glorious language go for nothing? God forbid that it should go for nothing. Arianism was at least so far Christian that it held aloft the Lord's example as the Son of Man, and never wavered in its worship of him as the Son of God. Whatever be the errors of its creed, whatever the scandals of its history, it was a power of life among the Northern nations. Let us give Arianism full honour for its noble work of missions in that age of deep despair which saw the dissolution of the ancient world.

<small>His doctrine</small>

<small>Its merits</small>

Nevertheless, this plausible Arian confession will not bear examination. It is only the philosophy of the day put into a Christian dress. It starts from the accepted belief that the unity of God excludes not only distinctions inside the divine nature, but also contact with the world. Thus the God of Arius is an unknown God, whose being is hidden in eternal mystery. No creature can reveal him, and he cannot reveal himself. But if he is not to touch the world, he needs a minister of creation.

<small>Its real meaning</small>

THE BEGINNINGS OF ARIANISM.

The Lord is rather such a minister than the conqueror of death and sin. No doubt he is the Son of God, and begotten before all worlds. Scripture is quite clear so far; but if he is distinct from the Father, he is not God; and if he is a Son, he is not co-eternal with the Father. And what is not God is creature, and what is not eternal is also creature. On both grounds, then, the Lord is only a creature; so that if he is called God, it is in a lower and improper sense; and if we speak of him as eternal, we mean no more than the eternity of all things in God's counsel. Far from sharing the essence of the Father, he does not even understand his own. Nay, more; he is not even a creature of the highest type. If he is not a sinner, (Scripture forbids at least *that* theory, though some Arians came very near it), his virtue is, like our own, a constant struggle of free-will, not the fixed habit which is the perfection and annulment of free-will. And now that his human soul is useless, we may as well simplify the incarnation into an assumption of human flesh and nothing more. The Holy Spirit bears to the Son a relation not unlike that of the Son to the Father. Thus the Arian trinity of divine persons forms a descending series, separated by infinite degrees of honour and glory, resembling the philosophical triad of orders of spiritual existence, extending outwards in concentric circles.

Indeed the system is heathen to the core. The Arian Christ is nothing but a heathen idol invented to maintain a heathenish Supreme in heathen isolation from the world. Never was a more illogical theory devised by the wit of man.

<small>Criticism of it.</small>

Arius proclaims a God of mystery, unfathomable to the
Son of God himself, and goes on to argue as if the divine
generation were no more mysterious than its human
type. He forgets first that metaphor would cease to
be metaphor if there were nothing beyond it; then
that it would cease to be true if its main idea were
misleading. He presses the metaphor of sonship as if
mere human relations could exhaust the meaning of
the divine; and soon works round to the conclusion
that it is no proper sonship at all. In his irreverent
hands the Lord's deity is but the common right of mankind,
his eternity no more than the beasts themselves
may claim. His clumsy logic overturns every doctrine
he is endeavouring to establish. He upholds the
Lord's divinity by making the Son of God a creature,
and then worships him to escape the reproach of
heathenism, although such worship, on his own showing,
is mere idolatry. He makes the Lord's manhood
his primary fact, and overthrows that too by refusing
the Son of Man a human soul. The Lord is neither
truly God nor truly man, and therefore is no true
mediator. Heathenism may dream of a true communion
with the Supreme, but for us there neither is
nor ever can be any. Between our Father and ourselves
there is a great gulf fixed, which neither he nor
we can pass. Now that we have heard the message
of the Lord, we know the final certainty that God is
darkness, and in him is no light at all. If this be
the sum of the whole matter, then revelation is a
mockery, and Christ is dead in vain.

Arius was but one of many who were measuring
the heights of heaven with their puny logic, and

sounding the deeps of Wisdom with the plummet of the schools. Men who agreed in nothing else agreed in this practical subordination of revelation to philosophy. Sabellius, for example, had reduced the Trinity to three successive manifestations of the one God in the Law, the Gospel, and the Church; yet even he agreed with Arius in a philosophical doctrine of the unity of God which was inconsistent with a real incarnation. Even the noble work of Origen had helped to strengthen the philosophical influences which were threatening to overwhelm the definite historic revelation. Tertullian had long since warned the churches of the danger; but a greater than Tertullian was needed now to free them from their bondage to philosophy. Are we to worship the Father of our spirits or the Supreme of the philosophers? Arius put the question: the answer came from Athanasius. Though his *De Incarnatione Verbi Dei* was written in early manhood, before the rise of Arianism, we can already see in it the firm grasp of fundamental principles which enabled him so thoroughly to master the controversy when it came before him. He starts from the beginning, with the doctrine that God is good and not envious, and that His goodness is shown in the creation, and more especially by the creation of man in the image of God, whereby he was to remain in bliss and live the true life, the life of the saints in Paradise. But when man sinned, he not only died, but fell into the entire corruption summed up in death; for this is the full meaning of the threat 'ye shall die with death.'[1] So things went on from

[1] Gen. ii. 17, LXX.

bad to worse on earth. The image of God was disappearing, and the whole creation going to destruction. What then was God to do? He could not take back his sentence that death should follow sin, and yet he could not allow the creatures of his love to perish. Mere repentance on man's side could not touch the law of sin; a word from God forbidding the approach of death would not reach the inner corruption. Angels could not help, for it was not in the image of angels that man was made. Only he who is himself the Life could conquer death. Therefore the immortal Word took human flesh and gave his mortal body for us all. It was no necessity of his nature so to do, but a pure outcome of his love to men and of the Father's loving purpose of salvation. By receiving in himself the principle of death he overcame it, not in his own person only, but in all of us who are united with him. If we do not yet see death abolished, it is now no more than the passage to our joyful resurrection. Our mortal human nature is joined with life in him, and clothed in the asbestos robe of immortality. Thus, and only thus, in virtue of union with him, can man become a sharer of his victory. There is no limit to the sovereignty of Christ in heaven and earth and hell. Wherever the creation has gone before, the issues of the incarnation must follow after. See, too, what he has done among us, and judge if his works are not the works of sovereign power and goodness. The old fear of death is gone. Our children tread it underfoot, our women mock at it. Even the barbarians have laid aside their warfare and their murders, and live at his bidding a new life of peace and purity. Heathenism

THE BEGINNINGS OF ARIANISM.

is fallen, the wisdom of the world is turned to folly, the oracles are dumb, the demons are confounded. The gods of all the nations are giving place to the one true God of mankind. The works of Christ are more in number than the sea, his victories are countless as the waves, his presence is brighter than the sunlight. 'He was made man that we might be made God.'[1]

The great persecution had been raging but a few years back, and the changes which had passed since then were enough to stir the enthusiasm of the dullest Christian. These splendid paragraphs are the song of victory over the defeat of the Pharaohs of heathenism and the deliverance of the churches from the house of bondage. 'Sing ye to the Lord, for he hath triumphed gloriously.' There is something in them higher than the fierce exultation of Lactantius over the sufferings of the dying persecutors, though that too is impressive. 'The Lord hath heard our prayers. The men who strove with God lie low; the men who overthrew his churches have themselves fallen with a mightier overthrow; the men who tortured the righteous have surrendered their guilty spirits under the blows of Heaven and in tortures well deserved though long delayed—yet delayed only that posterity might learn the full terrors of God's vengeance on his enemies.' There is none of this fierce joy in Athanasius, though he too had seen the horrors of the persecution, and some of his early teachers had perished in it. His eyes are fixed on the world-wide victory of the Eternal

Its significance

[1] Ath. *De Inc* 44: αὐτὸς γὰρ ἐνηνθρώπησεν ἵνα ἡμεῖς θεοποιηθῶμεν. Bold as this phrase is, it is not too bold a paraphrase of Heb. 11. 5-18.

Word, and he never lowers them to resent the evil
wrought by men of yesterday. Therefore neither
lapse of time nor multiplicity of trials could ever
quench in Athanasius the pure spirit of hope which
glows in his youthful work. Slight as our sketch
of it has been, it will be enough to show his combination of religious intensity with a speculative insight and a breadth of view reminding us of Origen.
If he fails to reach the mystery of sinlessness in man,
and is therefore not quite free from a Sabellianising
view of the Lord's humanity as a mere vesture of
his divinity, he at least rises far above the barren
logic of the Arians. We shall presently have to
compare him with the next great Eastern thinker,
Apollinarius of Laodicea.

Yet there were many men whom Arianism suited
by its shallowness. As soon as Christianity was
established as a lawful worship by the edict of Milan in 312, the churches were crowded with converts and inquirers of all sorts.

<small>Attraction of Arianism (1) For superficial thinkers</small>

A church which claims to be universal cannot pick
and choose like a petty sect, but must receive all
comers. Now these were mostly heathens with the
thinnest possible varnish of Christianity, and Arianism
enabled them to use the language of Christians without giving up their heathen ways of thinking. In
other words, the world was ready to accept the gospel
as a sublime monotheism, and the Lord's divinity was
the one great stumbling-block which seemed to hinder
its conversion. Arianism was therefore a welcome
explanation of the difficulty. Nor was the attraction
only for nominal Christians like these. Careless

thinkers—sometimes thinkers who were not careless —might easily suppose that Arianism had the best of such passages as 'The Lord created me,'[1] or 'The Father is greater than I.'[2] Athanasius constantly complains of the Arian habit of relying on isolated passages like these without regard to their context or to the general scope and drift of Scripture.

Nor was even this all. The Lord's divinity was a real difficulty to thoughtful men. They were still endeavouring to reconcile the philosophical idea of God with the fact of the incarnation. In point of fact, the two things are incompatible, and one or the other would have to be abandoned. The absolute simplicity of the divine nature is consistent with a merely external Trinity, or with a merely economic Trinity, with an Arian Trinity of one increate and two created beings, or with a Sabellian Trinity of three temporal aspects of the one God revealed in history; but not with a Christian Trinity of three eternal aspects of the divine nature, facing inward on each other as well as outward on the world. But this was not yet fully understood. The problem was to explain the Lord's distinction from the Father without destroying the unity of God. Sabellianism did it at the cost of his premundane and real personality, and therefore by common consent was out of the question. The Easterns were more inclined to theories of subordination, to distinctions of the derivatively from the absolutely divine, and to views of Christ as a sort of secondary God. Such theories do not really meet the

(2) To thoughtful men.

---

[1] Prov. viii 22, LXX mistranslation.
[2] John xiv 28.

difficulty. A secondary God is necessarily a second God. Thus heathenism still held the key of the position, and constantly threatened to convict them of polytheism. They could not sit still, yet they could not advance without remodelling their central doctrine of the divine nature to agree with revelation. Nothing could be done till the Trinity was placed inside the divine *nature*. But this is just what they could not for a long time see. These men were not Arians, for they recoiled in genuine horror from the polytheistic tendencies of Arianism; but they had no logical defence against Arianism, and were willing to see if some modification of it would not give them a foothold of some kind. To men who dreaded the return of Sabellian confusion, Arianism was at least an error in the right direction. It upheld the same truth as they—the separate personality of the Son of God—and if it went further than they could follow, it might still do service against the common enemy.

Thus the new theory made a great sensation at Alexandria, and it was not without much hesitation and delay that Alexander ventured to excommunicate his heterodox presbyter with his chief followers, like Pistus, Carpones, and the deacon Euzoius—all of whom we shall meet again. Arius was a dangerous enemy. His austere life and novel doctrines, his dignified character and championship of 'common sense in religion,' made him the idol of the ladies and the common people. He had plenty of telling arguments for them. 'Did the Son of God exist before his generation?' Or to the women, 'Were you a mother before you had a child?' He knew

The Beginnings of Arianism. 15

also how to cultivate his popularity by pastoral visiting —his enemies called it canvassing—and by issuing a multitude of theological songs 'for sailors and millers and wayfarers,' as one of his admirers says. So he set the bishop at defiance, and more than held his ground against him. The excitement spread to every village in Egypt, and Christian divisions became a pleasant subject for the laughter of the heathen theatres.

The next step was to secure outside support. Arius betook himself to Cæsarea in Palestine, and thence appealed to the Eastern churches generally.

And elsewhere

Nor did he look for help in vain. His doctrine fell in with the prevailing dread of Sabellianism, his personal misfortunes excited interest, his dignified bearing commanded respect, and his connection with the school of Lucian secured him learned and influential sympathy. Great Syrian bishops like those of Cæsarea, Tyre, and Laodicea gave him more or less encouragement; and when the old Lucianist Eusebius of Nicomedia held a council in Bithynia to demand his recall, it became clear that the controversy was more than a local dispute. Arius even boasted that the Eastern bishops agreed with him, 'except a few heretical and ill-taught men,' like those of Antioch and Jerusalem.

The Eastern Emperor, Licinius, let the dispute take its course. He was a rude old heathen soldier, and

Constantine's interference.

could only let it alone. If Eusebius of Nicomedia tried to use his influence in favour of Arius, he had small success. But when the battle of Chrysopolis laid the Empire at the feet of Constantine, it seemed time to get the question somehow settled.

323

CHAPTER II.

THE COUNCIL OF NICÆA.

FOR nearly twenty years after the middle of the third century, the Roman Empire seemed given over to
State of the   destruction. It is hard to say whether
Empire.   the provinces suffered more from the inroads
of barbarians who ravaged them almost at their will, or from the exactions of a mutinous soldiery who set up an emperor for almost every army; yet both calamities were surpassed by the horrors of a pestilence which swept away the larger part of mankind. There was little hope in an effete polytheism, still less in a corrupt and desponding society. The emperors could not even make head against their foreign enemies. Decius was killed in battle with the Goths, Valerian captured by the Persians. But the Teuton was not yet ready to be the heir of the world. Valerian left behind a school of generals who were able, even in those evil days, to restore the Empire to something like its former splendour. Claudius began by breaking the power of the Goths at Naissus in 269. Aurelian (270–275) made a firm peace with the Goths, and also recovered the provinces. Tetricus and Zenobia,

THE COUNCIL OF NICÆA.

the Gaulish Cæsar and the Syrian queen, adorned the triumph of their conqueror. The next step was for Diocletian (284–305) to reform the civil power and reduce the army to obedience. Unfortunately his division of the Empire into more manageable parts led to a series of civil wars, which lasted till its reunion by Constantine in 323. His religious policy was a still worse failure. Instead of seeing in Christianity the one remaining hope of mankind, he set himself at the end of his reign to stamp it out, and left his successors to finish the hopeless task. Here again Constantine repaired Diocletian's error. The edict of Milan in 312 put an end to the great persecution, and a policy of increasing favour soon removed all danger of Christian disaffection.

When Constantine stood out before the world as the patron of the gospel, he felt bound to settle the question of Arianism. In some ways he was well qualified for the task. There can be no doubt of his ability and earnestness, or of his genuine interest in Christianity. In political skill he was an overmatch for Diocletian, and his military successes were unequalled since the triumph of Aurelian. The heathens saw in him the restorer of the Empire, the Christians their deliverer from persecution. Even the feeling of a divine mission, which laid him so open to flattery, gave him also a keen desire to remedy the social misery around him; and in this he looked for help to Christianity. Amidst the horrors of Diocletian's persecution a conviction grew upon him that the power which fought the Empire with success must somehow come from the Supreme. Thus he slowly learned to recognise the God of the Christians in his father's God, and in the Sun-god's cross of light to see the cross of Christ. But in Christianity itself he found little more than a confirmation of natural religion. Therefore, with all his interest in the churches, he could not reach the secret of their inner life. Their imposing monotheism he fully appreciated, but the person of the Lord was surely a minor question. Constantine shared the heathen feelings of his time, so that the gospel to him was only a monotheistic heathenism. Thus Arianism came up to his idea of it, and the whole controversy seemed a mere affair of words.

But if he had no theological interest in the question, he could not overlook its political importance. Egypt was always a difficult province to manage; and if these Arian songs caused a bloody tumult in Alexandria, he could not let the Christians fight out their quarrels in the streets, as the Jews were used to do. The Donatists had given him trouble enough over a disputed election in Africa, and he did not want a worse than Donatist quarrel in Egypt. Nor was the danger confined to Egypt; it had already spread through the East. The unity of Christendom was at peril, and with it the support which the shattered Empire looked for from an undivided church. The state could treat with a definite organisation of churches, but not with miscellaneous gatherings of sectaries. The question must therefore be settled one way or the other, and settled at once. Which way it was decided mattered little, so that an end was made of the disturbance.

In this temper Constantine approached the difficulty. His first step was to send Hosius of Cordova to Alexandria with a letter to Alexander and Arius representing the question as a battle of words about mysteries beyond our reach. In the words of a modern writer, 'It was the excess of dogmatism founded upon the most abstract words in the most abstract region of human thought.' It had all arisen out of an over-curious question asked by Alexander, and a rash answer given by Arius. It was a childish quarrel and unworthy of sensible men like them, besides being very distressing to himself. Had the dispute been really trifling, such a letter might have had a chance of quieting it. Instead of this, the excitement grew worse.

His first attempt to settle it.

Constantine enlarged his plans. If Arian doctrine disturbed Alexandria, Meletius of Lycopolis was giving quite as much trouble about discipline farther up the Nile, and the old disputes about the time of Easter had never been effectually settled. There were also minor questions about the validity of baptism administered by the followers of Novatian and Paul of Samosata, and about the treatment of those who had denied the faith during the persecution of Licinius. Constantine, therefore, invited all Christian bishops inside and outside the Empire to meet him at Nicæa in Bithynia during the summer of 325, in order to make a final end of all the disputes which endangered the unity of Christendom. The 'city of victory' bore an auspicious name, and the restoration of peace was a holy service, and would be a noble preparation for the

Summons of the council

solemnities of the great Emperor's twentieth year upon the throne.

The idea of a general or œcumenical council (the words mean the same thing) may well have been Constantine's own. It bears the mark of a statesman's mind, and is of a piece with the rest of his life. Constantine was not thinking only of the questions to be debated. However these might be settled, the meeting could not fail to draw nearer to the state and to each other the churches of that great confederation which later ages have so often mistaken for the church of Christ. As regards Arianism, smaller councils had been a frequent means of settling smaller questions. Though Constantine had not been able to quiet the Donatists by means of the Council of Arles, he might fairly hope that the authority of such a gathering as this would bear down all resistance. If he could only bring the bishops to some decision, the churches might be trusted to follow it.

The first œcumenical council.

An imposing list of bishops answered Constantine's call. The signatures are 223, but they are not complete. The Emperor speaks of 300, and tradition gives 318, like the number of Abraham's servants, or like the mystic number[1] which stands for the cross of Christ. From the far west came his chief adviser for the Latin churches, the patriarch of councils, the old confessor Hosius of Cordova. Africa was represented by Caecilian of Carthage, round whose election the whole Donatist controversy had arisen, and a couple of presbyters answered for the apostolic and imperial see of Rome.

Its members.

---

[1] 318, in Greek τιη.

Of the thirteen great provinces of the Empire none was missing except distant Britain; but the Western bishops were almost lost in the crowd of Easterns. From Egypt came Alexander of Alexandria with his young deacon Athanasius, and the Coptic confessors Paphnutius and Potammon, each with an eye seared out, came from cities farther up the Nile. All these were resolute enemies of Arianism; its only Egyptian supporters were two bishops from the edge of the western desert. Syria was less unequally divided. If Eustathius of Antioch and Macarius of Ælia (we know that city better as Jerusalem) were on Alexander's side, the bishops of Tyre and Laodicea with the learned Eusebius of Cæsarea leaned the other way or took a middle course. Altogether there were about a dozen more or less decided Arianizers thinly scattered over the country from the slopes of Taurus to the Jordan valley. Of the Pontic bishops we need notice only Marcellus of Ancyra and the confessor Paul of Neocæsarea. Arianism had no friends in Pontus to our knowledge, and Marcellus was the busiest of its enemies. Among the Asiatics, however, there was a small but influential group of Arianizers, disciples of Lucian like Arius himself. Chief of these was Eusebius of Nicomedia, who was rather a court politician than a student like his namesake of Cæsarea, and might be expected to influence the Emperor as much as any one. With him went the bishops of Ephesus and Nicæa itself, and Maris of Chalcedon. The Greeks of Europe were few and unimportant, but on the outskirts of the Empire we find some names of great interest. James of Nisibis represented the old Syrian churches which spoke the Lord's own native language. Restaces the Armenian could remind the bishops that Armenia was in Christ before Rome, and had fought the persecutors in their cause. Theophilus the Goth might tell them the modest beginnings of Teutonic Christianity among his countrymen of the Crimean undercliff. John the Persian, who came from one or another of the many distant regions which bore the name of India, may dimly remind ourselves of the great Nestorian missions which one day were to make the Christian name a power in Northern China. Little as Eusebius of Cæsarea liked some issues of the council, he is full of genuine enthusiasm over his majestic roll of churches far and near, from the extremity of Europe to the farthest ends of Asia. Not without the Holy Spirit's guidance did that august assembly meet. Nor was its meeting a day of hope for the churches only, but also for the weary Empire. In that great crisis the deep despair of ages was forgotten. It might be that the power which had overcome the world could also cure its ancient sickness. Little as men could see into the issues of the future, the meaning of the present was beyond mistake. The new world faced the old, and all was ready for the league which joined the names of Rome and Christendom, and made the sway of Christ and Cæsar one.

It seems to have been understood that the council was to settle the question by drawing up a creed as a test for bishops. Here was a twofold novelty. In the first place, Christendom as a whole had as yet no written creed at all. The so-called Apostles' Creed may be older than 340, but then it first appears, and only as a personal confession

The idea of a test creed

THE COUNCIL OF NICÆA.

of the heretic Marcellus. Every church taught its catechumens the historic outlines of the faith, and referred to Scripture as the storehouse and final test of doctrine. But that doctrine was not embodied in forms of more than local currency. Thus different churches had varying creeds to form the basis of the catechumen's teaching, and placed varying professions in his mouth at baptism. Some of these were ancient, and some of widespread use, and all were much alike, for all were couched in Scripture language, variously modelled on the Lord's baptismal formula (Matt. xxviii. 19). At Jerusalem, for example, the candidate declared his faith

> in the Father;
> in the Son;
> in the Holy Spirit;
> and in one Baptism of Repentance.

The Roman form, as approximately given by Novatian in the middle of the third century, was,

> I believe in God the Father,
>   the Lord Almighty;
> in Christ Jesus his Son,
>   the Lord our God;
> and in the Holy Spirit.

Though these local usages were not disturbed, it was none the less a momentous step to draw up a document for all the churches. Its use as a test for bishops was a further innovation. Purity of doctrine was for a long time guarded by Christian public opinion. If a bishop taught novelties, the neighbouring churches (not the clergy only) met in conference on them, and refused his communion if they proved unsound. Of late years these conferences had been growing into formal councils of bishops, and the legal recognition of the churches by Gallienus had enabled them to take the further step of deposing false teachers. Aurelian had sanctioned this in the case of Paul of Samosata by requiring communion with the bishops of Rome and Italy as the legal test of Christian orthodoxy. But there were practical difficulties in this plan of government by councils. A strong party might dispute the sentence, or even get up rival councils to reverse it. The African Donatists had given Constantine trouble enough of this sort some years before; and now that the Arians were following their example, it was evident that every local quarrel would have an excellent chance of becoming a general controversy. In the interest, therefore, of peace and unity, it seemed better to adopt a written test. If a bishop was willing to sign it when asked, his subscription should be taken as a full reply to every charge of heresy which might be made against him. On this plan, whatever was left out of the creed would be deliberately left an open question in the churches. Whatever a bishop might choose to teach (Arianism, for example), he would have full protection, unless some clause of the new creed expressly shut it out. This is a point which must be kept in view when we come to estimate the conduct of Athanasius. Thus however Constantine hoped to make the bishops keep the peace over such trumpery questions as this of Arianism seemed to him. Had it been a trumpery question, his policy might have had

c 261.

272.

THE COUNCIL OF NICÆA. 25

some chance of lasting success. For the moment, at any rate, all parties accepted it, so that the council had only to settle the wording of the new creed.

The Arians must have come full of hope to the council. So far theirs was the winning side. They had a powerful friend at court in the Emperor's sister, Constantia, and an influential connection in the learned Lucianic circle. Reckoning also on the natural conservatism of Christian bishops, on the timidity of some, and on the simplicity or ignorance of others, they might fairly expect that if their doctrine was not accepted by the council, it would at least escape formal condemnation. They hoped, however, to carry all before them. An Arianizing creed was therefore presented by a score or so of bishops, headed by the courtier Eusebius of Nicomedia. They soon found their mistake. The Lord's divinity was not an open question in the churches. The bishops raised an angry clamour and tore the offensive creed in pieces. Arius was at once abandoned by nearly all his friends.

Arianism condemned.

This was decisive. Arianism was condemned almost unanimously, and nothing remained but to put on record the decision. But here began the difficulty. Marcellus and Athanasius wanted it put into the creed, but the bishops in general saw no need of this. A heresy so easily overcome could not be very dangerous. There were only half a dozen Arians left in the council, and too precise a definition might lead to dangers on the Sabellian side. At this point the historian Eusebius came forward. Though neither a great man nor a clear thinker, he was the

Eusebius proposes the creed of Cæsarea

most learned student of the East. He had been a confessor in the persecution, and now occupied an important see, and stood high in the Emperor's favour. With regard to doctrine, he held a sort of intermediate position, regarding the Lord not indeed as a creature, but as a secondary God derived from the will of the Father. This, as we have seen, was the idea then current in the East, that it is possible to find some middle term between the creature and the highest deity. To a man of this sort it seemed natural to fall back on the authority of some older creed, such as all could sign. He therefore laid before the council that of his own church of Cæsarea, as follows:—

We believe in one God, the Father Almighty,
> maker of all things, both visible and invisible;

And in one Lord Jesus Christ,
> the Word of God,
> God from God,
> light from light,
> life from life,
> the only-begotten Son,
> the first-born of all creation,
> begotten of the Father before all ages,—
> by whom also all things were made;

who for our salvation was made flesh,
> and lived among men,
> and suffered,
> and rose again the third day,
> and ascended to the Father,
> and shall come again in glory, to judge quick and dead;

And in the Holy Spirit.

THE COUNCIL OF NICÆA

Had the council been drawing up a creed for popular use, a short and simple document of this kind would have been suitable enough. The undecided bishops received it with delight. It contained none of the vexatious technical terms which had done all the mischief—nothing but familiar Scripture, which the least learned of them could understand. So far as Arianism might mean to deny the Lord's divinity, it was clearly condemned already, and the whole question might now be safely left at rest behind the ambiguities of the Cæsarean creed. So it was accepted at once. Marcellus himself could find no fault with its doctrine, and the Arians were glad now to escape a direct condemnation. But unanimity of this sort, which really decided nothing, was not what Athanasius and Marcellus wanted. They had not come to the council to haggle over compromises, but to cast out the blasphemer, and they were resolved to do it effectually.

Hardly a more momentous resolution can be found in history. The whole future of Christianity was determined by it; and we must fairly face the question whether Athanasius was right or not. Would it not have been every way better to rest satisfied with the great moral victory already gained? When heathens were pressing into the church in crowds, was that a suitable time to offend them with a solemn proclamation of the very doctrine which chiefly kept them back? It was, moreover, a dangerous policy to insist on measures for which even Christian opinion was not ripe, and it led directly to the gravest troubles in the churches—troubles of which no man then living was to see the end. The first

Persistence of Athanasius

half century of prelude was a war of giants; but the main contest opened at Nicæa is not ended yet, or like to end before the Lord himself shall come to end it. It was the decision of Athanasius which made half the bitterness between the Roman and the Teuton, between Christianity and Islam to this day. Even now it is the worst stumbling-block of Western unbelief. Many of our most earnest enemies would gladly forget their enmity if we would only drop our mysticism and admire with them a human Christ who never rose with power from the dead. But we may not do this thing. Christianity cannot make its peace with this world by dropping that message from the other which is its only reason for existence. Athanasius was clearly right. When Constantine had fairly put the question, they could not refuse to answer. Let the danger be what it might, they could not deliberately leave it open for Christian bishops (the creed was not for others) to dispute whether our Lord is truly God or not. Those may smile to whom all revelation is a vain thing; but it is our life, and we believe it is their own life too. If there is truth or even meaning in the gospel, this question of all others is most surely vital. Nor has history failed to justify Athanasius. That heathen age was no time to trifle with heathenism in the very citadel of Christian life. Fresh from the fiery trial of the last great persecution, whose scarred and mutilated veterans were sprinkled through the council-hall, the church of God was entering on a still mightier conflict with the spirit of the world. If their fathers had been faithful unto death or saved a people from the world, their sons would have to save the world itself and tame its Northern conquerors. Was that a time to say of Christ, 'But as for this man, we know not whence he is'?

Athanasius and his friends made a virtue of necessity, and disconcerted the plans of Eusebius by promptly accepting his creed. They were now able to propose a few amendments in it, and in this way they meant to fight out the controversy. It was soon found impossible to avoid a searching revision. Ill-compacted clauses invited rearrangement, and older churches, like Jerusalem or Antioch, might claim to share with Cæsarea the honour of giving a creed to the whole of Christendom. Moreover, several of the Cæsarean phrases seemed to favour the opinions which the bishops had agreed to condemn. 'First-born of all creation' does not necessarily mean more than that he existed before other things were made. 'Begotten before all worlds' is just as ambiguous, or rather worse, for the Arians understood 'begotten' to mean 'created.' Again, 'was made flesh' left it unsettled whether the Lord took anything more than a human body. These were serious defects, and the bishops could not refuse to amend them. After much careful work, the following was the form adopted:—

Revision of the Cæsarean creed

We believe in one God, the Father Almighty,
    maker of all things, both visible and invisible;
And in one Lord Jesus Christ,
    the Son of God,
      begotten of the Father, an only-begotten—
        that is, from the essence (*ousia*) of the Father—

The Nicene Creed.

God from God,
light from light,
true God from true God,
begotten, not made,
being of one essence (*homoousion*) with the Father,
by whom all things were made,
both things in heaven and things on earth:
who for us men and for our salvation came down and was made flesh,
was made man, suffered, and rose again the third day,
ascended into heaven,
cometh to judge quick and dead;
And in the Holy Spirit.

But those who say that
'there was once when he was not,' and
'before he was begotten he was not,' and
'he was made of things that were not,'
or maintain that the Son of God is of a different essence (*hypostasis or ousia* [1])
or created or subject to moral change or alteration—
these doth the Catholic and Apostolic Church anathematize.

It will be seen that the genuine Nicene Creed here given differs in almost every clause from the so-called Nicene Creed of our Communion Service.

Its doctrine

Leaving, however, the spurious Nicene Creed till we come to it, let us see how the genuine Nicene Creed dealt with Arianism. Its central phrases are the two which refer to essence. Now the *essence* of a thing is that by which it is what we suppose it to be. We look at it from various points of view, and ascribe to it first one quality and then another. Its *essence* from any one of these successive points of view is that by which it possesses the corresponding quality. About

[1] The two words are used as synonyms.

THE COUNCIL OF NICÆA. 31

this unknown something we make no assertion, so that we are committed to no theory whatever. Thus the *essence* of the Father *as God* (for this was the point of view) is that unknown and incommunicable something by which He is God. If therefore we explain St. John's 'an only-begotten who is God'[1] by inserting 'that is, from the *essence* of the Father,' we declare that the Divine Sonship is no accident of will, but belongs to the divine nature. It is not an outside matter of creation or adoption, but (so to speak) an organic relation inside that nature. The Father is no more God without the Son than the Son is God without the Father. Again, if we confess him to be *of one essence* with the Father, we declare him the common possessor with the Father of the one essence which no creature can share, and thus ascribe to him the highest deity in words which allow no evasion or reserve. The two phrases, however, are complementary. *From the essence* makes a clear distinction: *of one essence* lays stress on the unity. The word had a Sabellian history, and was used by Marcellus in a Sabellian sense, so that it was justly discredited as Sabellian. Had it stood alone, the creed would have been Sabellian; but at Nicæa it was checked by *from the essence*. When the later Nicenes, under Semiarian influence, came to give the word another meaning, the check was wisely removed.

Upon the whole, the creed is a cautious document. Though Arianism is attacked again in the clause *was made man*, which states that the Lord took something more than a human body, there

Its caution

[1] John i. 18 (the best reading, and certainly familiar in the Nicene age).

is no attempt to forestall later controversies by a further definition of the meaning of the incarnation. The abrupt pause after the mention of the Holy Spirit is equally significant, for the nature of his divinity was still an open question. Even the heretics are not cursed, for anathema in the Nicene age was no more than the penalty which to a layman was equivalent to the deposition of a cleric. It meant more when it was launched against the dead two hundred years later.

Our accounts of the debate are very fragmentary. Eusebius passes over an unpleasant subject, and Athanasius up and down his writings only tells us what he wants for his immediate purpose. Thus we cannot trace many of the Arian objections to the creed. Knowing, however, as we do that they were carefully discussed, we may presume that they were the standing difficulties of the next generation. These were four in number:—

(1.) 'From the essence' and 'of one essence' are materialist expressions, implying either that the Son is a separate part of the essence of the Father, or that there is some third essence prior to both. This objection was a difficulty in the East, and still more in the West, where 'essence' was represented by the materializing word *substantia*, from which we get our unfortunate translation 'of one substance.'

(2.) 'Of one essence' is Sabellian. This was true; and the defenders of the word did not seem to care if it was true. Marcellus almost certainly used incautious language, and it was many years before even Athanasius was fully awake to the danger from the Sabellian side.

The Council of Nicæa. 33

(3.) The words 'essence' and 'of one essence' are not found in Scripture. This is what seems to have influenced the bishops most of all.

(4.) 'Of one essence' is contrary to church authority. This also was true, for the word had been rejected as materializing by a large council held at Antioch in 269 against Paul of Samosata. The point, however, at present raised was not that it had been rejected for a good reason, but simply that it had been rejected; and this is an appeal to church authority in the style of later times. The question was one of Scripture against church authority. Both parties indeed accepted Scripture as supreme, but when they differed in its interpretation, the Arians pleaded that a word not sanctioned by church authority could not be made a test of orthodoxy. If tradition gave them a foothold (and none could deny it), they thought themselves entitled to stay; if Scripture condemned them (and there could be no doubt of that), Athanasius thought himself bound to turn them out. It was on the ground of Scripture that the fathers of Nicæa took their stand, and the works of Athanasius, from first to last, are one continuous appeal to Scripture. In this case he argues that if the disputed word is not itself Scripture, its meaning is. This was quite enough; but if the Arians chose to drag in antiquarian questions, they might easily be met on that ground also, for the word had been used or recognised by Origen and others at Alexandria. With regard to its rejection by the Syrian churches, he refuses all mechanical comparisons of date or numbers between the councils of Antioch and Nicæa, and endeavours to show that while Paul of Samosata had used the word in one sense, Arius denied it in another.

The council paused. The confessors in particular were an immense conservative force. If Hosius and Eustathius had been forward in attacking Arianism, few of them can have greatly wished to re-state the faith which had sustained them in their trial. Now the creed involved something like a revolution. The idea of a universal test was in itself a great change, best softened as much as might be. The insertion of a direct condemnation of Arianism was a still more serious step, and though the bishops had consented to it, they had not consented without misgiving. But when it was proposed to use a word of doubtful tendency, neither found in Scripture nor sanctioned by church authority, it would have been strange if they had not looked round for some escape.

Hesitation of the council.

Yet what escape was possible? Scripture can be used as a test if its authority is called in question, but not when its meaning is disputed. If the Arians were to be excluded, it was useless to put into the creed the very words whose plain meaning they were charged with evading. Athanasius gives an interesting account of this stage of the debate. It appears that when the bishops collected phrases from Scripture and set down that the Son is 'of God,' those wicked Arians said to each other, 'We can sign that, for we ourselves also are of God. Is it not written, All things are of God?'[1] So when the bishops saw their impious ingenuity, they put it more clearly, that the Son is

[1] 1 Cor. viii 6.

not only of God like the creatures, but of the essence of God. And this was the reason why the word 'essence' was put into the creed. Again, the Arians were asked if they would confess that the Son is not a creature, but the power and eternal image of the Father and true God. Instead of giving a straightforward answer, they were caught whispering to each other. 'This is true of ourselves, for we men are called the image and glory of God.[1] We too are eternal, for we who live are always.[2] And powers of God are many. Is He not the Lord of powers (hosts)? The locust and the caterpillar are actually "my great power which I sent among you."[3] He is true God also, for he became true God as soon as he was created.' These were the evasions which compelled the bishops to sum up the sense of Scripture in the statement that the Son is of one essence with the Father.

So far Athanasius. The longer the debate went on, the clearer it became that the meaning of Scripture could not be defined without going outside Scripture for words to define it. In the end, they all signed except a few. Many, however, signed with misgivings, and some almost avowedly as a formality to please the Emperor. 'The soul is none the worse for a little ink.' It is not a pleasant scene for the historian.

Acceptance of the creed

Eusebius of Cæsarea was sorely disappointed. Instead of giving a creed to Christendom, he received

---

[1] 1 Cor. xi. 7.
[2] 2 Cor. iv. 11; the impudence of the quotation is worth notice.
[3] Joel ii. 25 (army).

back his confession in a form which at first he could not sign at all. There was some ground for his complaint that, under pretence of inserting the single word *of one essence*, which our wise and godly Emperor so admirably explained, the bishops had in effect drawn up a composition of their own. It was a venerable document of stainless orthodoxy, and they had laid rude hands on almost every clause of it. Instead of a confession which secured the assent of all parties by deciding nothing, they forced on him a stringent condemnation, not indeed of his own belief, but of opinions held by many of his friends, and separated by no clear logical distinction from his own. But now was he to sign or not? Eusebius was not one of the hypocrites, and would not sign till his scruples were satisfied. He tells us them in a letter to the people of his diocese, which he wrote under the evident feeling that his signature needed some apology. First he gives their own Cæsarean creed, and protests his unchanged adherence to it. Then he relates its unanimous acceptance, subject to the insertion of the single word *of one essence*, which Constantine explained to be directed against materializing and unspiritual views of the divine generation. But it emerged from the debates in so altered a form that he could not sign it without careful examination. His first scruple was at *of the essence of the Father*, which was explained as not meant to imply any materializing separation. So, for the sake of peace, he was willing to accept it, as well as *of one essence*, now that he could do it with a good conscience. Similarly, *begotten, not made*,

<small>The letter of Eusebius</small>

THE COUNCIL OF NICÆA. 37

was explained to mean that the Son has nothing in common with the creatures made by him, but is of a higher essence, ineffably begotten of the Father. So also, on careful consideration, *of one essence with the Father* implies no more than the uniqueness of the Son's generation, and his distinctness from the creatures. Other expressions prove equally innocent.

Now that a general agreement had been reached, it was time for Constantine to interpose. He had summoned the council as a means of union, and enforced his exhortation to harmony by burning the letters of recrimination which the bishops had presented to him. To that text he still adhered. He knew too little of the controversy to have any very strong personal opinion, and the influences which might have guided him were divided. If Hosius of Cordova leaned to the Athanasian side, Eusebius of Nicomedia was almost Arian. If Constantine had any feeling in the matter—dislike, for example, of the popularity of Arius —he was shrewd enough not to declare it too hastily. If he tried to force a view of his own on the undecided bishops, he might offend half Christendom; but if he waited for the strongest force inside the council to assert itself, he might safely step in at the end to coerce the recusants. Therefore whatever pleased the council pleased the Emperor too. When they tore up the Arian creed, he approved. When they accepted the Cæsarean, he approved again. When the morally strong Athanasian minority urged the council to put in the disputed clauses, Constantine did his best to smooth the course of the debate. At last, always in the interest of unity, he proceeded to put pressure on

[margin: Constantine's interference]

the few who still held out. Satisfactory explanations were given to Eusebius of Cæsarea, and in the end they all signed but the two Egyptian Arians, Secundus of Ptolemais and Theonas of Marmarica. These were sent into exile, as well as Arius himself; and a qualified subscription from Eusebius of Nicomedia only saved him for the moment. An imperial rescript also branded the heretic's followers with the name of Porphyrians, and ordered his writings to be burnt. The concealment of a copy was to be a capital offence.

Other subjects decided by the council will not detain us long, though some of its members may have Close of the council. thought one or two of them quite as important as Arianism. The old Easter question was settled in favour of the Roman custom of observing, not the day of the Jewish passover in memory of the crucifixion, but a later Sunday in memory of the resurrection. For how, explains Constantine—how could we who are Christians possibly keep the same day as those wicked Jews? The council, however, was right on the main point, that the feasts of Christian worship are not to be tied to those of Judaism. The third great subject for discussion was the Meletian schism in Egypt, and this was settled by a liberal compromise. The Meletian presbyter might act alone if there was no orthodox presbyter in the place, otherwise he was to be a coadjutor with a claim to succeed if found worthy. Athanasius (at least in later times) would have preferred severer measures, and more than once refers to these with unconcealed disgust. The rest of the business disposed of, Constantine dismissed the bishops with a splendid feast, which Eusebius enthusiastically likens to the kingdom of heaven.

Let us now sum up the results of the council, so far as they concern Arianism. In one sense they were decisive. Arianism was so sharply condemned by the all but unanimous voice of Christendom, that nearly thirty years had to pass before it was openly avowed again. Conservative feeling in the West was engaged in steady defence of the great council; and even in the East its doctrine could be made to wear a conservative aspect as the actual faith of Christendom. On the other hand, were serious drawbacks. The triumph was rather a surprise than a solid victory. As it was a revolution which a minority had forced through by sheer strength of clearer thought, a reaction was inevitable when the half-convinced majority returned home. In other words, Athanasius had pushed the Easterns farther than they wished to go, and his victory recoiled on himself. But he could not retreat when once he had put the disputed words into the creed. Come what might, those words were irreversible. And if it was a dangerous policy which won the victory, the use made of it was deplorable. Though the exile of Arius and his friends was Constantine's work, much of the discredit must fall on the Athanasian leaders, for we cannot find that they objected to it either at the time or afterwards. It seriously embittered the controversy. If the Nicenes set the example of persecution, the other side improved on it till the whole contest threatened to degenerate into a series of personal quarrels and retaliations. The process was only checked by the common hatred of all parties to Julian, and by the growth of a better spirit among the Nicenes, as shown in the later writings of Athanasius.

CHAPTER III.

THE EUSEBIAN REACTION.

AT first sight the reaction which followed the Nicene council is one of the strangest scenes in history. The decision was clear and all but unanimous. Arianism seemed crushed for ever by the universal reprobation of the Christian world. Yet it instantly renewed the contest, and fought its conquerors on equal terms for more than half a century. A reaction like this is plainly more than a court intrigue. Imperial favour could do a good deal in the Nicene age, but no emperor could long oppose any clear and definite belief of Christendom. Nothing could be plainer than the issue of the council. How then could Arianism venture to renew the contest?

<small>The problem stated.</small>

The answer is, that though the belief of the churches was certainly not Arian, neither was it yet definitely Nicene. The dominant feeling both in East and West was one of dislike to change, which we may conveniently call conservatism. But here there was a difference. Heresies in the East had always gathered round the person of the Lord, and more than one had already partly occu-

<small>The reaction rather conservative than Arian</small>

pied the ground of Arianism. Thus Eastern conservatism inherited a doctrine from the last generation, and was inclined to look on the Nicene decisions as questionable innovations. The Westerns thought otherwise. Leaning on authority as they habitually did, they cared little to discuss for themselves an unfamiliar question. They could not even translate its technical terms into Latin without many misunderstandings. Therefore Western conservatism simply fell back on the august decisions of Nicæa. No later meeting could presume to rival 'the great and holy council' where Christendom had once for all pronounced the condemnation of Arianism. In short, East and West were alike conservative; but while conservatism in the East went behind the council, in the West it was content to start from it.

The Eastern reaction was therefore in its essence not Arian but conservative. Its leaders might be conservatives like Eusebius of Cæsarea, or court politicians like his successor, Acacius. They were never open Arians till 357.

Supported by influence of.
(1) Heathens.

The front and strength of the party was conservative, and the Arians at its tail were in themselves only a source of weakness. Yet they could enlist powerful allies in the cause of reaction. Heathenism was still a living power in the world. It was strong in numbers even in the East, and even stronger in the imposing memories of history. Christianity was still an upstart on Cæsar's throne. The favour of the gods had built up the Empire, and men's hearts misgave them that their wrath might overthrow it. Heathenism was still an established religion, the Emperor still its official

THE EUSEBIAN REACTION. 43

head. Old Rome was still devoted to her ancient deities, her nobles still recorded their priesthoods and augurships among their proudest honours, and the Senate itself still opened every sitting with an offering of incense on the altar of Victory. The public service was largely heathen, and the army too, especially its growing cohorts of barbarian auxiliaries. Education also was mostly heathen, turning on heathen classics and taught by heathen rhetoricians. Libanius, the teacher of Chrysostom, was also the honoured friend of Julian. Philosophy too was a great influence, now that it had leagued together all the failing powers of the ancient world against a rival not of this world. Its weakness as a moral force must not blind us to its charm for the imagination. Neoplatonism brought Egypt to the aid of Greece, and drew on Christianity itself for help. The secrets of philosophy were set forth in the mysteries of Eastern superstition. From the dim background of a noble monotheism the ancient gods came forth to represent on earth a majesty above their own. No waverer could face the terrors of that mighty gathering of infernal powers. And the Nicene age was a time of unsettlement and change, of half-beliefs and wavering superstition, of weakness and unclean frivolity. Above all, society was heathen to an extent we can hardly realise. The two religions were strangely mixed. The heathens on their side never quite understood the idea of worshipping one God only; while crowds of nominal Christians never asked for baptism unless a dangerous illness or an earthquake scared them, and thought it quite enough to show their faces in church once or twice a year.

Meanwhile, they lived just like the heathens round them, steeped in superstitions like their neighbours, attending freely their immoral games and dances, and sharing in the sins connected with them. Thus Arianism had many affinities with heathenism, in its philosophical idea of the Supreme, in its worship of a demigod of the vulgar type, in its rhetorical methods, and in its generally lower moral tone. Heathen influences therefore strongly supported Arianism.

The Jews also usually took the Arian side. They were still a power in the world, though it was long since Israel had challenged Rome to seventy years of internecine contest for the dominion of the East. But they had never forgiven her the destruction of Jehovah's temple. Half overcome themselves by the spell of the eternal Empire, they still looked vaguely for some Eastern deliverer to break her impious yoke. Still more fiercely they resented her adoption of the gospel, which indeed was no tidings of good-will or peace to them, but the opening of a thousand years of persecution. Thus they were a sort of caricature of the Christian churches. They made every land their own, yet were aliens in all. They lived subject to the laws of the Empire, yet gathered into corporations governed by their own. They were citizens of Rome, yet strangers to her imperial comprehensiveness. In a word, they were like a spirit in the body, but a spirit of uncleanness and of sordid gain. If they hated the Gentile, they could love his vices notwithstanding. If the old missionary zeal of Israel was extinct, they could still purvey impostures for the world. Jewish

(2) Jews

A.D. 66–135

THE EUSEBIAN REACTION. 45

superstitions were the plague of distant Spain, the despair of Chrysostom at Antioch. Thus the lower moral tone of Arianism and especially its denial of the Lord's divinity were enough to secure it a fair amount of Jewish support as against the Nicenes. At Alexandria, for example, the Jews were always ready for lawless outrage at the call of every enemy of Athanasius.

The court also leaned to Arianism. The genuine Arians, to do them justice, were not more pliant to imperial dictation than the Nicenes, but the genuine Arians were only one section of a motley coalition. Their conservative patrons and allies were laid open to court influence by their dread of Sabellianism; for conservatism is the natural home of the impatient timidity which looks round at every difficulty for a saviour of society, and would fain turn the whole work of government into a crusade against a series of scarecrows. Thus when Constantius turned against them, their chiefs were found wanting in the self-respect which kept both Nicene and Arian leaders from condescending to a battle of intrigue with such masters of the art as flourished in the palace. But for thirty years the intriguers found it their interest to profess conservatism. The court was as full of selfish cabals as that of the old French monarchy. Behind the glittering ceremonial on which the treasures of the world were squandered fought armies of place-hunters great and small, cooks and barbers, women and eunuchs, courtiers and spies, adventurers of every sort, for ever wresting the majesty of law to private favour, for ever aiming new oppressions at the men on

(3) The court.

whom the exactions of the Empire already fell with crushing weight. The noblest bishops, the ablest generals, were their fairest prey; and we have no surer witness to the greatness of Athanasius or Julian than the pertinacious hatred of this odious horde. Intriguers of this kind found it better to unsettle the Nicene decisions, on behalf of conservatism forsooth, than to maintain them in the name of truth. There were many ways of upsetting them, and each might lead to gain; only one of defending them, and that was not attractive.

Nor were Constantius and Valens without political reasons for their support of Arianism. We can see by the light of later history that the real centre of the Empire was the solid mass of Asia from the Bosphorus to Mount Taurus, and that Constantinople was its outwork on the side of Europe. In Rome on one side, Egypt and Syria on the other, we can already trace the tendencies which led to their separation from the orthodox Eastern Church and Empire. Now in the fourth century Asia was a stronghold of conservatism. There was a good deal of Arianism in Cappadocia, but we hear little of it in Asia. The group of Lucianists at Nicæa left neither Arian nor Nicene successors. The ten provinces of Asia 'verily knew not God' in Hilary's time; and even the later Nicene doctrine of Cappadocia was almost as much Semiarian as Athanasian. Thus Constantius and Valens pursued throughout an Asiatic policy, striking with one hand at Egypt, with the other at Rome. Every change in their action can be explained with reference to the changes of opinion in Asia.

(4) Asia.

THE EUSEBIAN REACTION. 47

Upon the whole, we may say that Arian hatred of the council would have been powerless if it had not rested on a formidable mass of conservative discontent, while the conservative discontent might have died away if the court had not supplied it with the means of action. If the decision lay with the majority, every initiative had to come from the court. Hence the reaction went on as long as these were agreed against the Nicene party; it was suspended as soon as Julian's policy turned another way, became unreal when conservative alarm subsided, and finally collapsed when Asia went over to the Nicene side.

Conclusion

We may now return to the sequel of the great council. If Constantine thought he had restored peace in the churches, he soon found out his mistake. The literary war began again almost where his summons had interrupted it. The creed was signed and done with and seemed forgotten. The conservatives hardly cared to be reminded of their half unwilling signatures. To Athanasius it may have been a watchword from the first, but it was not so to many others. In the West it was as yet almost unknown. Even Marcellus was more disposed to avoid all technical terms than to lay stress on those which the council sanctioned. Yet all parties had learned caution at Nicæa. Marcellus disavowed Sabellianism; Eusebius avoided Arianism, and nobody seems to have disowned the creed as long as Constantine lived.

Sequel of the council.

The next great change was at Alexandria. The bishop Alexander died in the spring of 328, and a stormy election followed. Its details are obscure, but the Nicene party put forward the deacon Athanasius, and consecrated him in spite of a determined opposition from Arians and Meletians. And now that we stand before the greatest of the Eastern fathers, let us see how his character and training fitted him to be the hero of the Arian controversy.

Athanasius bishop of Alexandria, A D 328.

Athanasius was a Greek by birth and education, Greek also in subtle thought and philosophic insight, in oratorical power and supple statesmanship. Though born almost within the shadow of the mighty temple of Serapis at Alexandria, he shows few signs of Coptic influence. Deep as is his feeling of the mystery of revelation, he has no love of mystery for its own sake, nothing of the Egyptian passion for things awful and mysterious. Even his style is clear and simple, without a trace of Egyptian involution and obscurity. We know nothing of his family, and cannot even date his birth for certain, though it must have been very near the year 297. He was, therefore, old enough to remember the worst days of the great persecution, which Maximin Daza kept up in Egypt as late as 313. Legend has of course been busy with his early life. According to one story, Alexander found him with some other boys at play, imitating the ceremonies of baptism—not a likely game for a youth of sixteen. Another story makes him a disciple of the great hermit Antony, who never existed. He may have been a lawyer for a time, but in any case his training was neither Coptic nor monastic, but Greek and scriptural, as became a scholar of Alexandria. There may be traces of Latin

Character of Athanasius

in his writings, but his allusions to Greek literature are such as leave no doubt that he had a liberal education. In his earliest works he refers to Plato; in later years he quotes Homer, and models his notes on Aristotle, his *Apology* to Constantius on Demosthenes. To Egyptian idolatry he seldom alludes. Scripture, however, is his chosen and familiar study, and few commentators have ever shown a firmer grasp of certain of its leading thoughts. He at least endeavoured (unlike the Arian text-mongers) to take in the context of his quotations and the general drift of Christian doctrine. Many errors of detail may be pardoned to a writer who so seldom fails in suggestiveness and width of view. In mere learning he was no match for Eusebius of Cæsarea, and even as a thinker he has a worthy rival in Hilary of Poitiers, while some of the Arian leaders were fully equal to him in political skill. But Eusebius was no great thinker, Hilary no statesman, and the Arian leaders were not men of truth. Athanasius, on the other hand, was philosopher, statesman, and saint in one. Few great men have ever been so free from littleness or weakness. At the age of twenty he had risen far above the level of Arianism and Sabellianism, and throughout his long career we catch glimpses of a spiritual depth which few of his contemporaries could reach. Above all things, his life was consecrated to a simple witness for truth. Athanasius is the hero of a mighty struggle, and the secret of his grandeur is his intense and vivid faith that the incarnation is a real revelation from the other world, and that its issues are for life and death supreme in heaven and earth and hell for evermore.

Such a bishop was sure to meet a bitter opposition,
and as sure to overcome it. Egypt soon became a
stronghold of the Nicene faith, for Athanasius
could sway the heart of Greek and Copt
alike. The pertinacious hatred of a few
was balanced by the enthusiastic admiration of the
many. The Meletians dwindled fast, the Arians faster
still. Nothing but outside persecution was needed now
to make Nicene orthodoxy the national faith of Egypt.

Early years of his rule at Alexandria.

It will be remembered that Eusebius of Nicomedia
was exiled shortly after the council. His disgrace was
not a long one. He had powerful friends
at court, and it was not very hard for a man
who had signed the creed to satisfy the Emperor of his
substantial orthodoxy. Constantine was not unforgiving, and policy as well as easy temper forbade him to
scrutinize too closely the professions of submission laid
before him. Once restored to his former influence at
court, Eusebius became the centre of intrigue against
the council. Old Lucianic friendships may have led
him on. Arius was a Lucianist like himself, and the
Lucianists had in vain defended him before the council.
Eusebius was the ablest of them, and had fared the
worst. He had strained his conscience to sign the
creed, and his compliance had not even saved him from
exile. We cannot wonder if he brought back a firm
determination to undo the council's hateful work. If
it was too dangerous to attack the creed itself, its
defenders might be got rid of one by one on various
pretexts. Such was the plan of operations.

Beginnings of the reaction.

A party was easily formed. The Lucianists were its
nucleus, and all sorts of malcontents gathered round

THE EUSEBIAN REACTION. 51

them. The Meletians of Egypt joined the coalition, and the unclean creatures of the palace rejoiced to hear of fresh intrigue. Above all, the conservatives gave extensive help. The charges against the Nicene leaders were often more than plausible, for men like the Cæsarean Eusebius dreaded Sabellianism, and Marcellus was practically Sabellian, and the others aiders and abettors of his misbelief. Some even of the darker charges may have had some ground, or at least have seemed truer than they were. Thus Eusebius had a very heterogeneous following, and it would be scant charity if we laid on all of them the burden of their leader's infamy.

Formation of the Eusebian coalition

They began with Eustathius of Antioch, an old confessor and a man of eloquence, who enjoyed a great and lasting popularity in the city. He was one of the foremost enemies of Arianism at Nicæa, and had since waged an active literary war with the Arianizing clique in Syria. In one respect they found him a specially dangerous enemy, for he saw clearly the important consequences of the Arian denial of the Lord's true human soul. Eustathius was therefore deposed (on obscure grounds) in 330, and exiled with many of his clergy to Thrace. The vacant see was offered to Eusebius of Cæsarea, and finally accepted by the Cappadocian Euphronius. But party spirit ran high at Antioch. The removal of Eustathius nearly caused a bloody riot, and his departure was followed by an open schism. The Nicenes refused to recognise Euphronius, and held their meetings apart, under the presbyter Paulinus, remaining without a bishop for more than thirty years.

Attacks on (1) Eustathius

52 *THE ARIAN CONTROVERSY.*

The system was vigorously followed up. Ten of the Nicene leaders were exiled in the next year or two. But Alexandria and Ancyra were the great strongholds of the Nicene faith, and the Eusebians still had to expel Marcellus and Athanasius. As Athanasius might have met a charge of heresy with a dangerous retort, it was found necessary to take other methods with him. Marcellus, however, was so far the foremost champion of the council, and he had fairly exposed himself to a doctrinal attack. Let us therefore glance at his theory of the incarnation.

(2) Marcellus.

Marcellus of Ancyra was already in middle life when he came forward as a resolute enemy of Arianism at Nicæa. Nothing is known of his early years and education, but we can see some things which influenced him later on. Ancyra was a strange diocese, full of uncouth Gauls and chaffering Jews, and overrun with Montanists and Manichees, and votaries of endless fantastic heresies and superstitions. In the midst of this turmoil Marcellus spent his life; and if he learned too much of the Galatian party spirit, he learned also that the gospel is wider than the forms of Greek philosophy. The speculations of Alexandrian theology were as little appreciated by the Celts of Asia as is the stately churchmanship of England by the Celts of Wales. They were the foreigner's thoughts, too cold for Celtic zeal, too grand for Celtic narrowness. Fickleness is not inconsistent with a true and deep religious instinct, and we may find something austere and high behind the ever-changing phases of spiritual excitement. Thus the ideal holiness of the church, upheld by Montanists and Novatians, attracted

Character of Marcellus

THE EUSEBIAN REACTION. 53

kindred spirits at opposite ends of the Empire, among the Moors of the Atlas and the Gauls of Asia. Such a people will have sins and scandals like its neighbours, but very little indifference or cynicism. It will be more inclined to make of Christian liberty an excuse for strife and debate. The zeal which carries the gospel to the loneliest mountain villages will also fill them with the jealousies of endless quarrelling sects; and the Gaul of Asia clung to his separatism with all the more tenacity for the consciousness that his race was fast dissolving in the broader and better world of Greece. Thus Marcellus was essentially a stranger to the wider movements of his time. His system is an appeal from Origen to St. John, from philosophy to Scripture. Nor can we doubt the high character and earnest zeal of the man who for years stood side by side with Athanasius. The more significant therefore is the failure of his bold attempt to cut the knot of controversy.

Marcellus then agreed with the Arians that the idea of sonship implies beginning and inferiority, so that a Son of God is neither eternal nor equal to the Father. When the Arians argued on both grounds that the Lord is a creature, the conservatives were content to reply that the idea of sonship excludes that of creation, and implies a peculiar relation to and origin from the Father. But their own position was weak. Whatever they might say, their secondary God was a second God, and their theory of the eternal generation only led them into further difficulties, for their concession of the Son's origin from the will of the Father made the Arian conclusion

<small>Doctrine of Marcellus.</small>

irresistible. Marcellus looked scornfully on a lame result like this. The conservatives had broken down because they had gone astray after vain philosophy. Turn we then to Scripture. 'In the beginning was,' not the Son, but the Word. It is no secondary or accidental title which St. John throws to the front of his Gospel, and repeats with deliberate emphasis three times over in the first verse. Thus the Lord is properly the Word of God, and this must govern the meaning of all such secondary names as the Son. Then he is not only the silent thinking principle which remains with God, but also the active creating power which comes forth too for the dispensation of the world. In this Sabellianizing sense Marcellus accepted the Nicene faith, holding that the Word is one with God as reason is one with man. Thus he explained the Divine Sonship and other difficulties by limiting them to the incarnation. The Word as such is pure spirit, and only became the Son of God by becoming the Son of Man. It was only in virtue of this humiliating separation from the Father that the Word acquired a sort of independent personality. Thus the Lord was human certainly on account of his descent into true created human flesh, and yet not merely human, for the Word remained unchanged. Not for its own sake was the Word incarnate, but merely for the conquest of Satan. 'The flesh profiteth nothing,' and even the gift of immortality cannot make it worthy of permanent union with the Word. God is higher than immortality itself, and even the immortal angels cannot pass the gulf which parts the creature from its Lord. That which is of the earth is useless for the age to come. Hence the human nature must be laid aside when its work is done and every hostile power overthrown. Then shall the Son of God deliver up the kingdom to the Father, that the kingdom of God may have no end; and then the Word shall return, and be for ever with the Father as before.

A universal cry of horror rose from the conservative ranks to greet the new Sabellius, the Jew and worse than Jew, the shameless miscreant who had forsworn the Son of God. Marcellus had confused together all the errors he could find. The faith itself was at peril if blasphemies like these were to be sheltered behind the rash decisions of Nicæa. So thought the conservatives, and not without a reason, though their panic was undignified from the first, and became a positive calamity when taken up by political adventurers for their own purposes. As far as doctrine went, there was little to choose between Marcellus and Arius. Each held firmly the central error of the conservatives, and rejected as illogical the modifications and side views by which they were finding their way to something better. Both parties, says Athanasius, are equally inconsistent. The conservatives, who refuse eternal being to the Son of God, will not endure to hear that his kingdom is other than eternal; while the Marcellians, who deny his personality outright, are equally shocked at the Arian limitation of it to the sphere of time. Nor had Marcellus escaped the difficulties of Arius. If, for example, the idea of an eternal Son is polytheistic, nothing is gained by transferring the eternity to an impersonal Word. If the generation of the Son is materializing, so also is the

The conservative panic.

coming forth of the Word. If the work of creation is unworthy of God, it may as well be delegated to a created Son as to a transitory Word. So far Athanasius. Indeed, to Marcellus the Son of God is a mere phenomenon of time, and even the Word is as foreign to the divine essence as the Arian Son. If the one can only reveal in finite measure, the other gives but broken hints of an infinity beyond. Instead of destroying Arianism by the roots, Marcellus had fallen into something very like Sabellianism. He reaches no true mediation, no true union of God and man, for he makes the incarnation a mere theophany, the flesh a useless burden, to be one day laid aside. The Lord is our Redeemer and the conqueror of death and Satan, but there is no room for a second Adam, the organic head of regenerate mankind. The redemption becomes a mere intervention from without, not also the planting of a power of life within, which will one day quicken our mortal bodies too.

Marcellus had fairly exposed himself to a doctrinal attack; other methods were used with Athanasius.

(3) Athanasius. They had material enough without touching doctrine. His election was disputed: Meletians and Arians complained of oppression: there were some useful charges of magic and political intrigue. At first, however, the Meletians could not even get a hearing from the Emperor. When Eusebius of Nicomedia took up their cause, they fared a little better. The attack had to be put off till the winter of 331, and was even then a failure. Their charges were partly answered by two presbyters of Athanasius who were on the spot; and when the bishop himself

was summoned to court, he soon completed their discomfiture. As Constantine was now occupied with the Gothic war, nothing more could be done till 334. When, however, Athanasius was ordered to attend a council at Cæsarea, he treated it as a mere cabal of his enemies, and refused to appear.

Next year the Eastern bishops gathered to Jerusalem to keep the festival of the thirtieth year of Constantine's reign and to dedicate his splendid church on Golgotha. But first it was a work of charity to restore peace in Egypt. A synod of about 150 bishops was held at Tyre, and this time the appearance of Athanasius was secured by peremptory orders from the Emperor. The Eusebians had the upper hand, though there was a strong minority. Athanasius brought nearly fifty bishops from Egypt, and others, like Maximus of Jerusalem and Alexander of Thessalonica, were willing to do justice. Athanasius was not accused of heresy, but, with more plausibility, of episcopal tyranny. His friends replied with reckless violence. Potammon aimed a bitter and unrighteous taunt at Eusebius of Cæsarea. 'You and I were once in prison for the faith. I lost an eye: how did you escape?' Athanasius might perhaps have been crushed if his enemies had kept up a decent semblance of truth and fairness. But nothing was further from their thoughts than an impartial trial. Scandal succeeded scandal, till the iniquity culminated in the dispatch of an openly partizan commission to superintend the manufacture of evidence in Egypt. Maximus of Jerusalem and Paphnutius left the council, saying that it was not good that old confessors like them

The Council of Tyre (335).

should share its evil deeds. The Egyptian bishops protested. Alexander of Thessalonica denounced the plot to the Emperor's representative. Athanasius himself took ship for Constantinople without waiting for the end of the farce, and the council condemned him by default. This done, the bishops went on to Jerusalem for the proper business of their meeting.

The concourse on Golgotha was a brilliant spectacle. Ten years had passed since the still unrivalled assembly at Nicæa, and the veterans of the last great persecution must have been deeply moved at their meeting once again in this world. The stately ceremonial suited Maximus and Eusebius much better than the noisy scene at Tyre, and may for the moment have soothed the swelling indignation of Potammon and Paphnutius. Constantine had once more plastered over the divisions of the churches with a general reconciliation, but this time Athanasius was condemned and Arius received to communion. The heretic had long since left his exile in Illyricum, though we cannot fix the date of his recall. However, one winter the Emperor invited Arius and his friend Euzoius to Constantinople, where they laid before him a short and simple confession of their faith. It said nothing of the disputed points, but was not unorthodox as far as it went. Nor were they bishops, that the Nicene creed should be forced upon them. Constantine was therefore satisfied, and now directed them to lay it before the bishops at Jerusalem, who duly approved of it and received its authors to communion. In order to complete the work of peace, Athanasius was condemned afresh on the return of the commission from

Assembly at Jerusalem.

THE EUSEBIAN REACTION. 59

Egypt, and proceedings were begun against Marcellus of Ancyra.

Meanwhile Constantine's dreams of peace were rudely dissipated by the sudden appearance of Athanasius before him in the streets of Constantinople. Whatever the bishops had done, they had plainly caused dissensions just when the Emperor was most anxious for harmony. An angry letter summoned the whole assembly straight to court. The meeting, however, was most likely dispersed before its arrival; at any rate, there came only a deputation of Eusebians. The result was unexpected. Instead of attempting to defend the council of Tyre, Eusebius of Nicomedia suddenly accused Athanasius of hindering the supply of corn for the capital. This was quite a new charge, and chosen with much skill. Athanasius was not allowed to defend himself, but summarily sent away to Trier in Gaul, where he was honourably received by the younger Constantine. On the other hand, the Emperor refused to let his place be filled up at Alexandria, and exiled the Meletian leader, John Archaph, 'for causing divisions.' To Constantinople came also Marcellus. He had kept away from the councils of Tyre and Jerusalem, and only came now to invite the Emperor's decision on his book. Constantine referred it as usual to the bishops, who promptly condemned it and deposed its author.

[side note: First exile of Athanasius]

There remained only the formal restoration of Arius to communion at Constantinople. But the heretic was taken ill suddenly, and died in the midst of a procession the evening before the day appointed. His enemies saw in his death a judgment

[side note: Death of Arius]

from heaven, and likened it to that of Judas. Only Athanasius relates it with reserve and dignity.

Upon the whole, Constantine had done his best for peace by leaving matters in an uneasy suspense which satisfied neither party. This seems the best explanation of his wavering. He had not turned Arian, for there is no sign that he ever allowed the decisions of Nicæa to be openly rejected inside the churches. Athanasius was not exiled for heresy, for there was no question of heresy in the case. The quarrel was ostensibly one of orthodox bishops, for Eusebius had signed the Nicene creed as well as Athanasius. Constantine's action seems to have been determined by Asiatic feeling. Had he believed the charge of delaying the corn-ships, he would have executed Athanasius at once. His conduct does not look like a real explosion of rage The merits of the case were not easy to find out, but the quarrel between Athanasius and the Asiatic bishops was a nuisance, so he sent him out of the way as a troublesome person. The Asiatics were not all of them either Arians or intriguers. It was not always furtive sympathy with heresy which led them to regret the heresiarch's expulsion for doctrines which he disavowed; neither was it always partizanship which could not see the innocence of Athanasius. Constantine's vacillation is natural if his policy was to seek for unity by letting the bishops guide him.

Policy of Constantine.

CHAPTER IV.

THE COUNCIL OF SARDICA.

CONSTANTINE'S work on earth was done. When the hand of death was on him, he laid aside the purple,
Death of Constantine, May 22, 337
and the ambiguous position of a Christian Cæsar with it, and passed away in the white robe of a simple convert. Long as he had been a friend to the churches, he had till now put off the elementary rite of baptism, in the hope one day to receive it in the waters of the Jordan, like the Lord himself. Darkly as his memory is stained with isolated crimes, Constantine must for ever rank among the greatest of the emperors; and as an actual benefactor of mankind, he stands alone among them. Besides his great services to the Empire in his own time, he gave the civilization of later days a new centre on the Bosphorus, beyond the reach of Goth or Vandal. Bulgarians and Saracens and Russians dashed themselves in pieces on the walls of Constantinople, and the strong arms of Western and crusading traitors were
A D 1204.
needed at last to overthrow the old bulwark which for so many centuries had guarded Christendom. Above all, it was Constantine who first

essayed the problem of putting a Christian spirit into the statecraft of the world. Hard as the task is even now, it was harder still in times when the gospel had not yet had time to form, as it were, an outwork of common feeling against some of the grosser sins. Yet whatever might be his errors, his legislation was a landmark for ever, because no emperor before him had been guided by a Christian sense of duty.

The sons of Constantine shared the Empire among them 'like an ancestral inheritance.' Thrace and Pontus had been assigned to their cousins, Dalmatius and Hannibalianus; but the army would have none but Constantine's own sons to reign over them. The whole house of Theodora perished in the tumult except two boys—Gallus and Julian, afterwards the apostate Emperor. Thus Constantine's sons were left in possession of the Empire. Constantine II. took Gaul and Italy, the legions of Syria secured the East for Constantius, and Italy and Illyricum were left for the share of the youngest, Constans.

<small>Division of the Empire.</small>

One of the first acts of the new Emperors was to restore the exiled bishops. Athanasius was released by the younger Constantine as soon as his father's death was known at Trier, and reached Alexandria in November 337, to the joy of both Greeks and Copts. Marcellus and the rest were restored about the same time, though not without much disturbance at Ancyra, where the intruding bishop Basil was an able man, and had formed a party.

<small>Recall of Athanasius, 337</small>

Let us now take a glance at the new Emperor of the East. Constantius had something of his father's character. In temperance and chastity, in love of

THE COUNCIL OF SARDICA. 63

letters and in dignity of manner, in social charm and pleasantness of private life, he was no unworthy son of Constantine; and if he inherited no splendid genius for war, he had a full measure of soldierly courage and endurance. Nor was the statesmanship entirely bad which kept the East in tolerable peace for four-and-twenty years. But Constantius was essentially a little man, in whom his father's vices took a meaner form. Constantine committed some great crimes, but the whole spirit of Constantius was corroded with fear and jealousy of every man better than himself. Thus the easy trust in unworthy favourites, which marks even the ablest of his family, became in Constantius a public calamity. It was bad enough when the uprightness of Constantine or Julian was led astray, but it was far worse when the eunuchs found a master too weak to stand alone, too jealous to endure a faithful counsellor, too easy-tempered and too indolent to care what oppressions were committed in his name, and without the sense of duty which would have gone far to make up for all his shortcomings. The peculiar repulsiveness of Constantius is not due to any flagrant personal vice, but to the combination of cold-blooded treachery, with the utter want of any inner nobleness of character. Yet he was a pious Emperor, too, in his own way. He loved the ecclesiastical game, and was easily won over to the Eusebian side. The growing despotism of the Empire and the personal unity of Constantius were equally suited by the episcopal timidity which cried for an arm of flesh to fight its battles. It is not easy to decide how far he acted on his own likings and

Character of Constantius.

superstitions, how far he merely let his flatterers lead him, or how far he saw political reasons for following them. In any case, he began with a thorough dislike of the Nicene council, continued for a long time to hold conservative language, and ended after some vacillation by adopting the vague Homoean compromise of 359.

Eusebian intrigue was soon resumed. Now that Constantine was dead, a schism could be set on foot at Alexandria; so the Arians were encouraged to hold assemblies of their own, and provided with a bishop in the person of Pistus, one of the original heretics deposed by Alexander. No fitter consecrator could be found for him than Secundus of Ptolemais, one of the two bishops who held out to the last against the council. The next move was the formal deposition of Athanasius by a council held at Antioch in the winter of 338. But there was still no charge of heresy—only old and new ones of sedition and intrigue, and a new argument, that after his deposition at Tyre he had forfeited all right to further justice by accepting a restoration from the civil power. This last was quite a new claim on behalf of the church, first used against Athanasius, and next afterwards for the ruin of Chrysostom, though it has since been made a pillar of the faith. Pistus was not appointed to the vacant see. The council chose Gregory of Cappadocia as a better agent for the rough work to be done. Athanasius was expelled by the apostate prefect Philagrius, and Gregory installed by military violence in his place. Scenes of outrage were enacted all over Egypt.

Second exile of Athanasius, Lent, 339

THE COUNCIL OF SARDICA

Athanasius fled to Rome. Thither also came Marcellus of Ancyra, and ejected clerics from all parts of the East. Under the rule of Constans they might meet with justice. Bishop Julius at once took the position of an arbiter of Christendom. He received the fugitives with a decent reserve, and invited the Eusebians to the council they had already asked him to hold. For a long time there came no answer from the East. The old heretic Carpones appeared at Rome on Gregory's behalf, but the envoys of Julius were detained at Antioch till January 340, and at last dismissed with an unmannerly reply. After some further delay, a synod of about fifty bishops met at Rome the following autumn. The cases were examined, Marcellus and Athanasius acquitted, and it remained for Julius to report their decision to the Easterns.

Athanasius and Marcellus at Rome.

His letter is one of the ablest documents of the entire controversy. Nothing can be better than the calm and high judicial tone in which he lays open every excuse of the Eusebians. He was surprised, he says, to receive so discourteous an answer to his letter. But what was their grievance? If it was his invitation to a synod, they could not have much confidence in their cause. Even the great council of Nicæa had decided (and not without the will of God) that the acts of one synod might be revised by another. Their own envoys had asked him to hold a council, and the men who set aside the decisions of Nicæa by using the services of heretics like Secundus Pistus and Carpones could hardly claim finality for their own doings at Tyre.

The letter of Julius

Their complaint that he had given them too short a notice would have been reasonable if the appointed day had found them on the road to Rome. 'But this also, beloved, is only an excuse.' They had detained his envoys for months at Antioch, and plainly did not mean to come. As for the reception of Athanasius, it was neither lightly nor unjustly done. The Eusebian letters against him were inconsistent, for no two of them ever told the same story; and they were, moreover, contradicted by letters in his favour from Egypt and elsewhere. The accused had come to Rome when summoned, and waited for them eighteen months in vain, whereas the Eusebians had uncanonically appointed an utter stranger in his place at Alexandria, and sent him with a guard of soldiers all the way from Antioch to disturb the peace of Egypt with horrible outrages. With regard to Marcellus, he had denied the charge of heresy and presented a very sound confession of his faith. The Roman legates at Nicæa had also borne witness to the honourable part he had taken in the council. Thus the Eusebians could not say that Athanasius and Marcellus had been too hastily received at Rome. Rather their own doings were the cause of all the troubles, for complaints of their violence came in from all parts of the East. The authors of these outrages were no lovers of peace, but of confusion. Whatever grievance they might have against Athanasius, they should not have neglected the old custom of writing first to Rome, that a legitimate decision might issue from the apostolic see. It was time to put an end to these scandals, as they would have to answer for them in the day of judgment.

THE COUNCIL OF SARDICA. 67

Severe as the letter is, it contrasts well with the disingenuous querulousness of the Eusebians. Nor is Julius unmindful to press as far as possible the claims of the Roman see. His one serious mistake was in supporting Marcellus. No doubt old services at Nicæa counted heavily in the West. His confession too was innocent enough, being very nearly our so-called Apostles' Creed, here met for the first time in history.[1] Knowing, however, what his doctrine was, we must admit that the Easterns were right in resenting its deliberate approval at Rome.

Criticism of it.

The Eusebians replied in the summer of 341, when ninety bishops met at Antioch to consecrate the Golden Church, begun by Constantine. The character of the council is an old question of dispute. Hilary calls it a meeting of saints, and its canons have found their way into the authoritative collections; yet its chief work was to confirm the deposition of Athanasius and to draw up creeds in opposition to the Nicene. Was it Nicene or Arian? Probably neither, but conservative. The Eusebians seem to have imitated Athanasius in pressing a creed (this time an Arianizing one) on unwilling conservatives, but only to have succeeded in making great confusion. This was a new turn of their policy, and not a hopeful one. Constantine's death indeed left them free to try if they could replace the Nicene creed by something else; but the friends of

Council of the dedication at Antioch (341)

---

[1] It has even been ascribed to Marcellus; but it seems a little older. Its apostolic origin is of course absurd. The legend cannot be traced beyond the last quarter of the fourth century.

Athanasius could accept no substitute, and even the conservatives could hardly agree to make the Lord's divinity an open question. The result was twenty years of busy creed-making, and twenty more of confusion, before it was finally seen that there was no escape from the dilemma which had been decisive at Nicæa

The Eusebians began by offering a meagre and evasive creed, much like the confession of Arius and Euzoius, prefacing it with a declaration that they were not followers of Arius, but his independent adherents. They overshot their mark, for the conservatives were not willing to go so far as this, and, moreover, had older standards of their own. Instead, therefore, of drawing up a new creed, they put forward a work of the venerated martyr Lucian of Antioch. Such it was said to be, and such in the main it probably was, though the anathemas must have been added now. This Lucianic formula then is essentially conservative, but leans much more to the Nicene than to the Arian side. Its central clause declares the Son of God 'not subject to moral change or alteration, but the unvarying image of the deity and essence and power and counsel and glory of the Father,' while its anathemas condemn 'those who say that there was once *a time* when the Son of God was not, or that he is a creature *as one of the creatures*.' These are strong words, but they do not in the least shut out Arianism. No doubt the phrase 'unvarying image of the essence' means that there is no change of essence in passing from the Father to the Son, and

The Lucianic creed (second of Antioch)

THE COUNCIL OF SARDICA. 69

is therefore logically equivalent to 'of one essence' (*homoousion*); but the conservatives meant nothing more than 'of like essence' (*homoiousion*), which is consistent with great unlikeness in attributes. The anathemas also are the Nicene with insertions which might have been made for the very purpose of letting the Arians escape. However, the conservatives were well satisfied with the Lucianic creed, and frequently refer to it with a veneration akin to that of Athanasius for the Nicene. But the wire-pullers were determined to upset it. The confession next presented by Theophronius of Tyana was more to their mind, for it contained a direct anathema against "Marcellus and those who communicated with him." It secured a momentary approval, but the meeting broke up without adopting it. The Lucianic formula remained the creed of the council.

Defeated in a free council, the wire-pullers a few months later assembled a cabal of their own, and drew up a fourth creed, which a deputation of notorious Arianizers presented to Constans in Gaul as the genuine work of the council. *The fourth creed* It seems to have suited them better than the Lucianic, for they repeated it with increasing series of anathemas at Philippopolis in 343, at Antioch the next year, and at Sirmium in 351. We can see why it suited them. While in substance it is less opposed to Arianism than the Lucianic, its wording follows the Nicene, even to the adoption of the anathemas in a weakened form. Upon the whole, it is a colourless document, which left all questions open.

The wording of the creed of Tyana was a direct blow

at Julius of Rome, and is of itself enough to show that its authors were no lovers of peace. But Western suspicion was already roused by the issue of the Lucianic creed. There could no longer be any doubt that the Nicene faith was the real object of attack. Before the Eastern envoys reached Constans in Gaul, he had already written to his brother (Constantine II. was now dead) to demand a new general council. Constantius was busy with the Persian war, and could not refuse; so it was summoned to meet in the summer of 343. To the dismay of the Eusebians, the place chosen was Sardica in Dacia, just inside the dominions of Constans. After their failure with the Eastern bishops at Antioch, they could not hope to control the Westerns in a free council.

Constans demands a council.

To Sardica the bishops came. The Westerns were about ninety-six in number, 'with Hosius of Cordova for their father,' bringing with him Athanasius and Marcellus, and supported by the chief Westerns—Gratus of Carthage, Protasius of Milan, Maximus of Trier, Fortunatian of Aquileia, and Vincent of Capua, the old Roman legate at Nicæa. The Easterns, under Stephen of Antioch and Acacius of Cæsarea, the disciple and successor of Eusebius, were for once outnumbered. They therefore travelled in one body, more than seventy strong, and agreed to act together. They began by insisting that the deposition of Marcellus and Athanasius at Antioch should be accepted without discussion. Such a demand was absurd. There was no reason why the deposition at Antioch should be accepted blindly

Council of Sardica (343).

rather than the acquittal at Rome. At any rate, the council had an express commission to re-open the whole case, and indeed had met for no other purpose; so, if they were not to do it, they might as well go home. The Westerns were determined to sift the whole matter to the bottom, but the Eusebians refused to enter the council. It was in vain that Hosius asked them to give their proofs, if it were only to himself in private. In vain he promised that if Athanasius was acquitted, and they were still unwilling to receive him, he would take him back with him to Spain. The Westerns began the trial: the Easterns left Sardica by night in haste. They had heard, forsooth, of a victory on the Persian frontier, and must pay their respects to the Emperor without a moment's delay.

Once more the charges were examined and the accused acquitted. In the case of Marcellus, it was found that the Eusebians had misquoted his book, setting down opinions as his own which he had only put forward for discussion. Thus it was not true that he had denied the eternity of the Word in the past or of his kingdom in the future. Quite so: but the eternity of the Sonship is another matter. This was the real charge against him, and he was allowed to evade it. Though doctrinal questions lay more in the background in the case of Athanasius, one party in the council was for issuing a new creed in explanation of the Nicene. The proposal was wisely rejected. It would have made the fatal admission that Arianism had not been clearly condemned at Nicæa, and thrown on the Westerns the

Acquittal of Marcellus and Athanasius.

72 THE ARIAN CONTROVERSY.

odium of innovation. All that could be done was to pass a series of canons to check the worst scandals of late years. After this the council issued its encyclical and the bishops dispersed.

Meanwhile the Easterns (such was their haste) halted for some weeks at Philippopolis to issue their own encyclical, falsely dating it from Sardica. They begin with their main argument, that the acts of councils are irreversible. Next they recite the charges against Athanasius and Marcellus, and the doings of the Westerns at Sardica. Hereupon they denounce Hosius, Julius, and others as associates of heretics and patrons of the detestable errors of Marcellus. A few random charges of gross immorality are added, after the Eusebian custom. They end with a new creed, the fourth of Antioch, with some verbal changes, and seven anathemas instead of two.

Rival council of Philippopolis.

The quarrel of East and West seemed worse than ever. The Eusebians had behaved discreditably enough, but they had at least frustrated the council, and secured a recognition of their creed from a large body of Eastern conservatives. So far they had been fairly successful, but the next move on their side was a blunder and worse. When the Sardican envoys, Vincent of Capua and Euphrates of Cologne, came eastward in the spring of 344, a harlot was brought one night into their lodgings. Great was the scandal when the plot was traced up to the Eusebian leader, Stephen of Antioch. A new council was held, by which Stephen was deposed and Leontius the Lucianist, himself the subject of an

The fifth creed of Antioch (344).

THE COUNCIL OF SARDICA. 73

old scandal, was raised to the vacant see. The fourth creed of Antioch was also re-issued with a few changes, but followed by long paragraphs of explanation. The Easterns adhered to their condemnation of Marcellus, and joined with him his disciple Photinus of Sirmium, who had made the Lord a mere man like the Ebionites. On the other hand, they condemned several Arian phrases, and insisted in the strongest manner on the mutual, inseparable, and, as it were, organic union of the Son with the Father in a single deity.

This conciliatory move cleared the way for a general suspension of hostilities. Stephen's crime had discredited the whole gang of Eastern court intriguers who had made the quarrel. Nor were the Westerns unreasonable. Though they still upheld Marcellus, they frankly gave up and condemned Photinus. Meanwhile Constans pressed the execution of the decrees of Sardica, and Constantius, with a Persian war on his hands, could not refuse. The last obstacle was removed by the death of Gregory of Cappadocia in 345. It was not till the third invitation that Athanasius returned. He had to take leave of his Italian friends, and the Emperor's letters were only too plainly insincere. However, Constantius received him graciously at Antioch, ordered all the charges against him to be destroyed, and gave him a solemn promise of full protection for the future. Athanasius went forward on his journey, and the old confessor Maximus assembled the bishops of Palestine to greet him at Jerusalem. But his entry into Alexandria (Oct. 346) was the crowning triumph of his life. For miles along the road the great city streamed out to

Return of Athanasius (Oct. 346)

meet him with enthusiastic welcome, and the jealous
police of Constantius could raise no tumult to mar the
universal harmony of that great day of national rejoicing.

The next few years were an uneasy interval of suspense rather than of peace, for the long contest had so
far decided nothing. If the Nicene exiles
were restored, the Eusebian disturbers were
not deposed. Thus while Nicene animosity was not
satisfied, the standing grounds of conservative distrust
were not removed. Above all, the return of Athanasius was a personal humiliation for Constantius, which
he was not likely to accept without watching his opportunity for a final struggle to decide the mastery of
Egypt. Still there was tolerable quiet for the present.
The court intriguers could do nothing without the
Emperor, and Constantius was occupied first with the
Persian war, then with the civil war against Magnentius.
If there was not peace, there was a fair amount of quiet
till the Emperor's hands were freed by the death of
Magnentius in 353.

Interval of rest (346–353)

The truce was hollow and the rest precarious, but
the mere cessation of hostilities was not without its
influence. As Nicenes and conservatives
were fundamentally agreed on the reality of
the Lord's divinity, minor jealousies began
to disappear when they were less busily encouraged.
The Eusebian phase of conservatism, which emphasised
the Lord's personal distinction from the Father, was
giving way to the Semiarian, where stress was rather
laid on his essential likeness to the Father. Thus 'of
a like essence' (*homoiousion*) and 'like in all things'
became more and more the watchwords of conservatism.

Modification of Nicene position.

THE COUNCIL OF SARDICA. 75

The Nicenes, on the other side, were warned by the excesses of Marcellus that there was some reason for the conservative dread of the Nicene 'of one essence' (*homoousion*) as Sabellian. The word could not be withdrawn, but it might be put forward less conspicuously, and explained rather as a safe and emphatic form of the Semiarian 'of like essence' than as a rival doctrine. Henceforth it came to mean absolute likeness of attributes rather than common possession of the divine essence. Thus by the time the war is renewed, we can already foresee the possibility of a new alliance between Nicenes and conservatives.

We see also the rise of a new and more defiant Arian school, more in earnest than the older generation, impatient of their shuffling diplomacy and less pliant to court influences. Aetius was a man of learning and no small dialectic skill, who had passed through many troubles in his earlier life and been the disciple of several scholars, mostly of the Lucianic school, before he came to rest in a clear and simple form of Arianism. Christianity without mystery seems to have been his aim. The Anomœan leaders took their stand on the doctrine of Arius himself, and dwelt with most emphasis on its most offensive aspects. Arius had long ago laid down the absolute unlikeness of the Son to the Father, but for years past the Arianizers had prudently softened it down. Now, however, 'unlike' became the watchword of Aetius and Eunomius, and their followers delighted to shock all sober feeling by the harshest and profanest declarations of it. The scandalous jests of Eudoxius must have given deep offence to thousands; but the great novelty

Rise of Anomœans

of the Anomœan doctrine was its audacious self-sufficiency. Seeing that Arius was illogical in regarding the divine nature as incomprehensible, and yet reasoning as if its relations were fully explained by human types, the Anomœans boldly declared that it is no mystery at all. If the divine essence is simple, man can perfectly understand it. 'Canst thou by searching find out God?' Yes, and know him quite as well as he knows me. Such was the new school of Arianism—presumptuous and shallow, quarrelsome and heathenising, yet not without a directness and a firmness of conviction which gives it a certain dignity in spite of its wrangling and irreverence. Its conservative allies it despised for their wavering and insincerity; to its Nicene opponents it repaid hatred for hatred, and flung back with retorted scorn their denial of its right to bear the Christian name.

We may now glance at the state of the churches at Jerusalem and Antioch during the years of rest.

<small>Illustration from the state of (1) Jerusalem</small> Jerusalem had been a resort of pilgrims since the days of Origen, and Helena's visit shortly after the Nicene council had fully restored it to the dignity of a holy place. We still have the itinerary of a nameless pilgrim who found his way from Bordeaux to Palestine in 333. The great church, however, of the Resurrection, which Constantine built on Golgotha, was only dedicated by the council of 335. The *Catecheses* of Cyril are a series of sermons on the creed, delivered to the catechumens of that church in 348. If it is not a work of any great originality, it will show us all the better what was passing in the minds of men of practical

The Council of Sardica.

and simple piety, who had no taste for the controversies of the day. All through it we see the earnest pastor who feels that his strength is needed to combat the practical immoralities of a holy city (Jerusalem was a scandal of the age), and never lifts his eyes to the wild scene of theological confusion round him but in fear and dread that Antichrist is near. 'I fear the wars of the nations; I fear the divisions of the churches; I fear the mutual hatred of the brethren. Enough concerning this. God forbid it come to pass in our days; yet let us be on our guard. Enough concerning Antichrist.' Jews, Samaritans, and Manichees are his chief opponents; yet he does not forget to warn his hearers against the teaching of Sabellius and Marcellus, 'the dragon's head of late arisen in Galatia.' Arius he sometimes contradicts in set terms, though without naming him. Of the Nicenes too, we hear nothing directly, but they seem glanced at in the complaint that whereas in former times heresy was open, the church is now full of secret heretics. The Nicene creed again he never mentions, but we cannot mistake the allusion when he tells his hearers that their own Jerusalem creed was not put together by the will of men, and impresses on them that every word of it can be proved by Scripture. But the most significant feature of his language is its close relation to that of the dated creed of Sirmium in 359. Nearly every point where the latter differs from the Lucianic is one specially emphasized by Cyril. If then the Lucianic creed represents the earlier conservatism, it follows that Cyril expresses the later views which had to be conciliated in 359.

The condition of Antioch under Leontius (344–357) is equally significant. The Nicene was quite as strong in the city as Arianism had ever been at Alexandria. The Eustathians formed a separate and strongly Nicene congregation under the presbyter Paulinus, and held their meetings outside the walls. Athanasius communicated with them on his return from exile, and agreed to give the Arians a church in Alexandria, as Constantius desired, if only the Eustathians were allowed one inside the walls of Antioch. His terms were prudently declined, for the Arians were a minority even in the congregation of Leontius. The old Arian needed all his caution to avoid offence. 'When this snow melts,' touching his white head, 'there will be much mud.' Nicenes and Arians made a slight difference in the doxology; and Leontius always dropped his voice at the critical point, so that nobody knew what he said. This policy was successful in keeping out of the Eustathian communion not only the indifferent multitude, but also many whose sympathies were clearly Nicene, like the future bishops Meletius and Flavian. But they always considered him an enemy, and the more dangerous for the contrast of his moderation with the reckless violence of Macedonius at Constantinople. His appointments were Arianizing, and he gave deep offence by the ordination of his old disciple, the detested Aetius. So great was the outcry that Leontius was forced to suspend him. The opposition was led by two ascetic laymen, Flavian and Diodorus, who both became distinguished bishops in later time. Orthodox feeling was nourished by a vigorous use of hymns and by all-night services at the

(2.) Antioch.

THE COUNCIL OF SARDICA.

tombs of the martyrs. As such practices often led to great abuses, Leontius may have had nothing more in view than good order when he directed the services to be transferred to the church.

The case of Antioch was not exceptional. Arians and Nicenes were still parties inside the church rather than distant sects. They still used the same prayers and the same hymns, still worshipped in the same buildings, still commemorated the same saints and martyrs, and still considered themselves members of the same church. The example of separation set by the Eustathians at Antioch and the Arians at Alexandria was not followed till a later stage of the controversy, when Diodorus and Flavian on one side, and the Anomœans on the other, began to introduce their own peculiarities into the service. And if the bitterness of intestine strife was increased by a state of things which made every bishop a party nominee, there was some compensation in the free intercourse of parties afterwards separated by barriers of persecution. Nicenes and Arians in most places mingled freely long after Leontius was dead, and the Novatians of Constantinople threw open their churches to the victims of Macedonius in a way which drew his persecution on themselves, and was remembered in their favour even in the next century by liberal men like the historian Socrates.

State of parties

CHAPTER V.

THE VICTORY OF ARIANISM.

MEANWHILE new troubles were gathering in the West.
While the Eastern churches were distracted with the
The West crimes or wrongs of Marcellus and Athana-
(337-350) sius, Europe remained at peace from the
Atlantic to the frontier of Thrace. The western
frontier of Constantius was also the western limit of
the storm. Hitherto its distant echoes had been very
faintly heard in Gaul and Spain; but now the time
was come for Arianism to invade the tranquil obscurity
of the West.

Constans was not ill-disposed, and for some years
ruled well and firmly. Afterwards—it may be that
Magnentian his health was bad—he lived in seclusion
war, 350-353 with his Frankish guards, and left his subjects to the oppression of unworthy favourites. Few
regretted their weak master's fate when the army of
Gaul proclaimed Magnentius Augustus (January 350).
But the memory of Constantine was still a power
which could set up emperors and pull them down.
The old general Vetranio at Sirmium received the
purple from Constantine's daughter, and Nepotianus

claimed it at Rome as Constantine's nephew. The Magnentian generals scattered the gladiators of Nepotianus, and disgraced their easy victory with slaughter and proscription. The ancient mother of the nations never forgave the intruder who had disturbed her queenly rest with civil war and filled her streets with bloodshed. Meantime Constantius came up from Syria, won over the legions of Illyricum, reduced Vetranio to a peaceful abdication, and pushed on with augmented forces towards the Julian Alps, there to decide the strife between Magnentius and the house of Constantine. Both parties tried the resources of intrigue; but while Constantius won over the Frank Silvanus from the Western camp, the envoys of Magnentius, who sounded Athanasius, gained nothing from the wary Greek. The decisive battle was fought near Mursa, on the Save (September 28, 351). Both armies well sustained the honour of the Roman name, and it was only after a frightful slaughter that the usurper was thrown back on Aquileia. Next summer he was forced to evacuate Italy, and in 353 his destruction was completed by a defeat in the Cottian Alps. Magnentius fell upon his sword, and Constantius remained the master of the world.

The Eusebians were not slow to take advantage of the confusion. The fires of controversy in the East were smouldering through the years of rest, so that it was no hard task to make them blaze afresh. As the recall of the exiles was only due to Western pressure, the death of Constans cleared the way for further operations. Marcellus and Photinus were again deposed by a council held at Sirmium in

Renewal of the contest

351. Ancyra was restored to Basil, Sirmium given to Germinius of Cyzicus. Other Eastern bishops were also expelled, but there was no thought of disturbing Athanasius for the present. Constantius more than once repeated to him his promise of protection.

Magnentius had not meddled with the controversy. He was more likely to see in it the chance of an ally at Alexandria than a matter of practical interest in the West. As soon, however, as Constantius was master of Gaul, he set himself to force on the Westerns an indirect condemnation of the Nicene faith in the person of Athanasius. Any direct approval of Arianism was out of the question, for Western feeling was firmly set against it by the council of Nicæa. Liberius of Rome followed the steps of his predecessor Julius. Hosius of Cordova was still the patriarch of Christendom, while Paulinus of Trier, Dionysius of Milan, and Hilary of Poitiers proved their faith in exile. Mere creatures of the palace were no match for men like these. Doctrine was therefore kept in the background. Constantius began by demanding from the Western bishops a summary and lawless condemnation of Athanasius. No evidence was offered; and when an accuser was asked for, the Emperor himself came forward, and this at a time when Athanasius was ruling Alexandria in peace on the faith of his solemn and repeated promises of protection.

The Western bishops.

A synod was held at Arles as soon as Constantius was settled there for the winter. The bishops were not unwilling to take the Emperor's word for the crimes of Athanasius, if only the court party cleared

THE VICTORY OF ARIANISM. 83

itself from the suspicion of heresy by anathematizing
Arianism. Much management and no little violence
was needed to get rid of this condition;
but in the end the council yielded. Even
the Roman legate, Vincent of Capua, gave
way with the rest, and Paulinus of Trier alone stood
firm, and was sent away to die in exile.

Council of Arles (Oct 353)

There was a sort of armed truce for the next two
years. Liberius of Rome disowned the weakness of
his legates and besought the Emperor to
hold a new council. But Constantius was
busy with the barbarians, and had to leave
the matter till he came to Milan in the autumn of
355. There Julian was invested with the purple and
sent as Cæsar to drive the Alemanni out of Gaul, or,
as some hoped, to perish in the effort. The council,
however, was for a long time quite unmanageable, and
only yielded at last to open violence. Dionysius of
Milan, Eusebius of Vercellæ, and Lucifer of Calaris in
Sardinia were the only bishops who had to be exiled.

Council of Milan (Oct. 355)

The appearance of Lucifer is enough to show that
the contest had entered on a new stage. The lawless tyranny of Constantius had roused an
aggressive fanaticism which went far beyond
the claim of independence for the church. In daunt-
less courage and determined orthodoxy Lucifer may
rival Athanasius himself, but any cause would have been
disgraced by his narrow partisanship and outrageous
violence. Not a bad name in Scripture but is turned
to use. Indignation every now and then supplies the
place of eloquence, but more often common sense itself
is almost lost in the weary flow of vulgar scolding and

Lucifer of Calaris

interminable abuse. He scarcely condescends to reason, scarcely even to state his own belief, but revels in the more congenial occupation of denouncing the fires of damnation against the disobedient Emperor.

The victory was not to be won by an arm of flesh like this. Arianism had an enemy more dangerous than Lucifer. From the sunny land of Aquitaine, the firmest conquest of Roman civilization in Atlantic Europe, came Hilary of Poitiers, the noblest representative of Western literature in the Nicene age. Hilary was by birth a heathen, and only turned in ripe manhood from philosophy to Scripture, coming before us in 355 as an old convert and a bishop of some standing. He was by far the deepest thinker of the West, and a match for Athanasius himself in depth of earnestness and massive strength of intellect. But Hilary was a student rather than an orator, a thinker rather than a statesman like Athanasius. He had not touched the controversy till it was forced upon him, and would much have preferred to keep out of it. But when once he had studied the Nicene doctrine and found its agreement with his own conclusions from Scripture, a clear sense of duty forbade him to shrink from manfully defending it. Such was the man whom the brutal policy of Constantius forced to take his place at the head of the Nicene opposition. As he was not present at Milan, the courtiers had to silence him some other way. In the spring of 356 they exiled him to Asia, on some charge of conduct 'unworthy of a bishop, or even of a layman.'

Hilary of Poitiers.

Meanwhile Hosius of Cordova was ordered to Sirmium and there detained. Constantius was not

The Victory of Arianism. 85

ashamed to send to the rack the old man who had been a confessor in his grandfather's days, more than fifty years before. He was brought at last to communicate with the Arianizers, but even in his last illness refused to condemn Athanasius. After this there was but one power in the West which could not be summarily dealt with The grandeur of Hosius was merely personal, but Liberius claimed the universal reverence due to the apostolic and imperial See of Rome. It was a great and wealthy church, and during the last two hundred years had won a noble fame for world-wide charity. Its orthodoxy was without a stain; for whatever heresies might flow to the great city, no heresy had ever issued thence. The strangers of every land who found their way to Rome were welcomed from St. Peter's throne with the majestic blessing of a universal father. 'The church of God which sojourneth in Rome' was the immemorial counsellor of all the churches; and now that the voice of counsel was passing into that of command, Bishop Julius had made a worthy use of his authority as a judge of Christendom. Such a bishop was a power of the first importance now that Arianism was dividing the Empire round the hostile camps of Gaul and Asia. If the Roman church had partly ceased to be a Greek colony in the Latin capital, it was still the connecting link of East and West, the representative of Western Christianity to the Easterns, and the interpreter of Eastern to the Latin West. Liberius could therefore treat almost on the footing of an independent sovereign. He would not condemn Athanasius unheard, and after so many

<small>Hosius and Liberius.</small>

acquittals. If Constantius wanted to reopen the case, he must summon a free council, and begin by expelling the Arians. To this demand he firmly adhered. The Emperor's threats he disregarded, the Emperor's gifts he flung out of the church. It was not long before Constantius was obliged to risk the scandal of seizing and carrying off the bishop of Rome.

Athanasius was still at Alexandria. When the notaries tried to frighten him away, he refused to take their word against the repeated written promises of protection he had received from Constantius himself. Duty as well as policy forbade him to believe that the most pious Emperor could be guilty of any such treachery. So when Syrianus, the general in Egypt, brought up his troops, it was agreed to refer the whole question to Constantius Syrianus broke the agreement. On a night of vigil (Feb. 8, 356) he surrounded the church of Theonas with a force of more than five thousand men. The whole congregation was caught as in a net. The doors were broken open, and the troops pressed up the church. Athanasius fainted in the tumult; yet before they reached the bishop's throne its occupant had somehow been safely conveyed away.

Third exile of Athanasius (356)

If the soldiers connived at the escape of Athanasius, they were all the less disposed to spare his flock. The outrages of Philagrius and Gregory were repeated by Syrianus and his successor, Sebastian the Manichee; and the evil work went on apace after the arrival of the new bishop in Lent 357. George of Cappadocia is said to have been before this a pork-contractor for the army, and is certainly no

George of Cappadocia.

THE VICTORY OF ARIANISM. 87

credit to Arianism. Though Athanasius does injustice
to his learning, there can be no doubt that he was a
thoroughly bad bishop. Indiscriminate oppression of
Nicenes and heathens provoked resistance from the fierce
populace of Alexandria. George escaped with difficulty
from one riot in August 358, and was fairly driven from
the city by another in October.

Meanwhile Athanasius had disappeared from the
eyes of men. A full year after the raid of Syrianus,
Athanasius in exile (356-362) he was still unconvinced of the Emperor's
treachery. Outrage after outrage might
turn out to be the work of underlings. Constantine
himself had not despised his cry for justice, and if he
could but stand before the son of Constantine, his
presence might even yet confound the gang of eunuchs.
Even the weakness of Athanasius is full of nobleness.
Not till the work of outrage had gone on for many
months was he convinced. But then he threw off all
restraint. Even George the pork-contractor is not
assailed with such a storm of merciless invective as
his holiness Constantius Augustus. George might sin
'like the beasts who know no better,' but no wicked-
ness of common mortals could attain to that of the new
Belshazzar, of the Lord's anointed 'self-abandoned to
eternal fire.'

The exile governed Egypt from his hiding in the
desert. Alexandria was searched in vain; in vain the
Political meaning of his exile. malice of Constantius pursued him to the
court of Ethiopia. Letter after letter issued
from his inaccessible retreat to keep alive
the indignation of the faithful, and invisible hands
conveyed them to the farthest corners of the land.

Constantius had his revenge, but it shook the Empire to its base. It was the first time since the fall of Israel that a nation had defied the Empire in the name of God. It was a national rising, none the less real for not breaking out in formal war. This time Greeks and Copts were united in defence of the Nicene faith, so that the contest was at an end when the Empire gave up Arianism. But the next breach was never healed. Monophysite Egypt was a dead limb of the Empire, and the Roman power beyond Mount Taurus fell before the Saracens because the provincials would not lift a hand to fight for the heretics of Chalcedon.

The victory seemed won when the last great enemy was driven into the desert, and the intriguers hasted to the spoil. They forgot that the West was only overawed for the moment, that Egypt was devoted to its patriarch, that there was a strong opposition in the East, and that the conservatives, who had won the battle for them, were not likely to take up Arianism at the bidding of their unworthy leaders. Amongst the few prominent Eusebians of the West were two disciples of Arius who held the neighbouring bishoprics of Mursa and Singidunum, the modern Belgrade. Valens and Ursacius were young men in 335, but old enough to take a part in the infamous Egyptian commission of the council of Tyre. Since that time they had been well to the front in the Eusebian plots. In 347, however, they had found it prudent to make their peace with Julius of Rome by confessing the falsehood of their charges against Athanasius. Of late they had been active on

<small>The Sirmian manifesto (357)</small>

THE VICTORY OF ARIANISM. 89

the winning side, and enjoyed much influence with Constantius. Thinking it now safe to declare more openly for Arianism, they called a few bishops to Sirmium in the summer of 357, and issued a manifesto of their belief for the time being, to the following general effect. 'We acknowledge one God the Father, also His only Son, Jesus Christ our Lord. But two Gods must not be preached. The Father is without beginning, invisible, and in every respect greater than the Son, who is subject to Him together with the creatures. The Son is born of the Father, God of God, by an inscrutable generation, and took flesh or body, that is, man, through which he suffered. The words *essence, of the same essence, of like essence*, ought not to be used, because they are not found in Scripture, and because the divine generation is beyond our understanding.' Here is something to notice besides the repeated hints that the Son is no better than a creature. It was a new policy to make the mystery in the manner of the divine generation an excuse for ignoring the fact. In this case the plea of ignorance is simply impertinent.

The Sirmian manifesto is the turning-point of the whole contest. Arianism had been so utterly crushed at Nicæa that it had never again till now appeared in a public document. Henceforth the conservatives were obliged in self-defence to look for a Nicene alliance against the Anomœans. Suspicions and misunderstandings, and at last mere force, delayed its consolidation till the reign of Theodosius, but the Eusebian coalition fell to pieces the moment Arianism ventured to have a policy of its own.

<small>Its results in general</small>

Ursacius and Valens had blown a trumpet which was heard from one end of the Empire to the other. Its avowal of Arianism caused a stir even in the West. Unlike the creeds of Antioch, it was a Western document, drawn up in Latin by Western bishops. The spirit of the West was fairly roused, now that the battle was clearly for the faith. The bishops of Rome, Cordova, Trier, Poitiers, Toulouse, Calaris, Milan, and Vercellæ were in exile, but Gaul was now partly shielded from persecution by the varying fortunes of Julian's Alemannic war. Thus everything increased the ferment. Phœbadius of Agen took the lead, and a Gaulish synod at once condemned the 'blasphemy.'

(1) In the West

If the Sirmian manifesto disturbed the West, it spread dismay through the ranks of the Eastern conservatives. Plain men were weary of the strife, and only the fishers in troubled waters wanted more of it. Now that Marcellus and Photinus had been expelled, the Easterns looked for rest. But the Sirmian manifesto opened an abyss at their feet. The fruits of their hard-won victories over Sabellianism were falling to the Anomœans. They must even defend themselves, for Ursacius and Valens had the Emperor's ear. As if to bring the danger nearer home to them, Eudoxius the new bishop of Antioch, and Acacius of Cæsarea convened a Syrian synod, and sent a letter of thanks to the authors of the manifesto.

(2) In the East.

Next spring came the conservative reply from a knot of twelve bishops who had met to consecrate a new church for Basil of Ancyra. But its weight was far beyond its numbers. Basil's name stood high for learn-

THE VICTORY OF ARIANISM. 91

ing, and he more than any man could sway the vacillating Emperor. Eustathius of Sebastia was another man of mark. His ascetic eccentricities, long ago condemned by the council of Gangra, were by this time forgotten or considered harmless. Above all, the synod represented most of the Eastern bishops. Pontus indeed was devoted to conservatism, and the decided Arianizers were hardly more than a busy clique even in Asia and Syria. Its decisions show the awkwardness to be expected from men who have had to make a sudden change of front, and exhibit well the transition from Eusebian to Semiarian conservatism. They seem to start from the declaration of the Lucianic creed, that the Lord's sonship is not an idle name. Now if we reject materialising views of the Divine Sonship, its primary meaning will be found to lie in similarity of essence. On this ground the Sirmian manifesto is condemned. Then follow eighteen anathemas, alternately aimed at Aetius and Marcellus. The last of these condemns the Nicene *of one essence*—clearly as Sabellian, though no reason is given.

Synod of Ancyra (Lent, 358).

The synod broke up. Basil and Eustathius went to lay its decisions before the court at Sirmium. To conciliate the Nicenes, they left out the last six anathemas of Ancyra. They were just in time to prevent Constantius from declaring for Eudoxius and the Anomœans. Peace was made before long on Semiarian terms. A collection was made of the decisions against Photinus and Paul of Samosata, together with the Lucianic creed, and signed by Liberius of Rome, by Ursacius and Valens, and by all

Victory of the Semiarians

the Easterns present. Liberius had not borne exile well. He had already signed some still more compromising document, and is denounced for it as an apostate by Hilary and others. However, he was now allowed to return to his see.

The Semiarians had won a complete victory. Their next step was to throw it away. The Anomœan leaders were sent into exile. After all, these Easterns only wanted to replace one tyranny by another. The exiles were soon recalled, and the strife began again with more bitterness than ever.

The Semiarian failure

Here was an opening for a new party. Semiarians, Nicenes, and Anomœans were equally unable to settle this interminable controversy. The Anomœans indeed almost deserved success for their boldness and activity, but pure Arianism was hopelessly discredited throughout the Empire. The Nicenes had Egypt and the West, but they could not at present overcome the court and Asia. The Semiarians might have mediated, but men who began with persecutions and wholesale exiles were not likely to end with peace. In this deadlock better men than Ursacius and Valens might have been tempted to try some scheme of compromise. But existing parties left no room for anything but vague and spacious charity. If we may say neither *of one essence* nor *of like essence*, nor yet *unlike*, the only course open is to say *like*, and forbid nearer definition. This was the plan of the new Homœan party formed by Acacius in the East, Ursacius and Valens in the West.

Rise of the Homœans.

Parties began to group themselves afresh. The

THE VICTORY OF ARIANISM. 93

Anomœans leaned to the side of Acacius. They had no favour to expect from Nicenes or Semiarians, but to the Homœans they could look for connivance at least. The Semiarians were therefore obliged to draw still closer to the Nicenes. Here came in Hilary of Poitiers. If he had seen in exile the worldliness of too many of the Asiatic bishops, he had also found among them men of a better sort who were in earnest against Arianism, and not so far from the Nicene faith as was supposed. To soften the mutual suspicions of East and West, he addressed his *De Synodis* to his Gaulish friends about the end of 358. In it he reviews the Eusebian creeds to show that they are not indefensible. He also compares the rival phrases *of one essence* and *of like essence*, to shew that either of them may be rightly or wrongly used. The two, however, are properly identical, for there is no likeness but that of unity, and no use in the idea of likeness but to exclude Sabellian confusion. Only the Nicene phrase guards against evasion, and the other does not.

New relations of parties

Now that the Semiarians were forced to treat with their late victims on equal terms, they agreed to hold a general council. Both parties might hope for success. If the Homœan influence was increasing at court, the Semiarians were strong in the East, and could count on some help from the Western Nicenes. But the court was resolved to secure a decision to its own mind. As a council of the whole Empire might have been too independent, it was divided. The Westerns were to meet at Ariminum in Italy, the Easterns at Seleucia in Isauria; and in

Summons for a council.

case of disagreement, ten deputies from each side were to hold a conference before the Emperor. A new creed was also to be drawn up before their meeting and laid before them for acceptance.

The 'Dated Creed' was drawn up at Sirmium on Pentecost Eve 359, by a small meeting of Homœan and Semiarian leaders. Its prevailing character is conservative, as we see from its repeated appeals to Scripture, its solemn tone of reverence for the person of the Lord, its rejection of the word *essence* for the old conservative reason that it is not found in Scripture, and above all, from its elaborate statement of the eternity and mysterious nature of the divine generation. The chief clause however is, 'But we say that the Son is *like* the Father in all things, as the Scriptures say and teach.' Though the phrase here is Homœan, the doctrine seems at first sight Semiarian, not to say Nicene. In point of fact, the clause is quite ambiguous. First, if the comma is put before *in all things*, the next words will merely forbid any extension of the likeness beyond what Scripture allows; and the Anomœans were quite entitled to sign it with the explanation that for their part they found very little likeness taught in Scripture. Again, likeness in all things cannot extend to essence, for all likeness which is not identity implies difference, if only the comparison is pushed far enough. So the Anomœans argued, and Athanasius accepts their reasoning. The Semiarians had ruined their position by attempting to compromise a fundamental contradiction. The whole contest was lowered to a court intrigue. There is grandeur in the flight of Athanasius, dignity in the exile of Eunomius; but the conservatives fell ignobly and unregretted, victims of their own violence and unprincipled intrigue.

After signing the creed, Ursacius and Valens went on to Ariminum, with the Emperor's orders to the council to take doctrinal questions first, and not to meddle with Eastern affairs. They found the Westerns waiting for them, to the number of more than two hundred. The bishops were in no courtly temper, and the intimidation was not likely to be an easy task. They had even refused the usual imperial help for the expenses of the journey. Three British bishops only accepted it on the ground of poverty. The new creed was very ill received; and when the Homœan leaders refused to anathematize Arianism, they were deposed, 'not only for their present conspiracy to introduce heresy, but also for the confusion they had caused in all the churches by their repeated changes of faith.' The last clause was meant for Ursacius and Valens. The Nicene creed was next confirmed, and a statement added in defence of the word *essence*. This done, envoys were sent to report at court and ask the Emperor to dismiss them to their dioceses, from which they could ill be spared. Constantius was busy with his preparations for the Persian war, and refused to see them. They were sent to wait his leisure, first at Hadrianople, then at the neighbouring town of Nicé (chosen to cause confusion with Nicæa), where Ursacius and Valens induced them to sign a revision of the dated creed. The few changes made in it need not detain us.

Meanwhile the Easterns met at Seleucia near the Cilician coast. It was a fairly central spot, and easy of access from Egypt and Syria by sea, but otherwise most unsuitable. It was a mere fortress, lying in a rugged country, where the spurs of Mount Taurus reach the sea. Around it were the ever-restless maranders of Isauria. They had attacked the place that very spring, and it was still the headquarters of the army sent against them. The choice of such a place is as significant as if a Pan-Anglican synod were called to meet at the central and convenient port of Souakin. Naturally the council was a small one. Of the 150 bishops present, about 110 were Semiarians. The Acacians and Anomœans were only forty, but they had a clear plan and the court in their favour. As the Semiarian leaders had put themselves in a false position by signing the dated creed, the conservative defence was taken up by men of the second rank, like Silvanus of Tarsus and the old soldier Eleusius of Cyzicus. With them, however, came Hilary of Poitiers, who, though still an exile, had been summoned with the rest. The Semiarians welcomed him, and received him to full communion.

Eastern Council at Seleucia.

Next morning the first sitting was held. The Homœans began by proposing to abolish the Nicene creed in favour of one to be drawn up in scriptural language. Some of them argued in defiance of their own Sirmian creed, that 'generation is unworthy of God. The Lord is creature, not Son, and his generation is nothing but creation.' The Semiarians, however, had no objection to the Nicene creed beyond the obscurity of the word *of one essence*. The still more important

Its proceedings.

of the essence of the Father seems to have passed without remark. Towards evening Silvanus of Tarsus proposed to confirm the Lucianic creed, which was done next morning by the Semiarians only. On the third day the Count Leonas, who represented the Emperor, read a document given him by Acacius, which turned out to be the dated creed revised afresh and with a new preface. In this the Homœans say that they are far from despising the Lucianic creed, though it was composed with reference to other controversies. The words *of one essence* and *of like essence* are next rejected because they are not found in Scripture, and the new Anomœan *unlike* is anathematized—'but we clearly confess the likeness of the Son to the Father, according to the apostle's words, Who is the image of the invisible God.' There was a hot dispute on the fourth day, when Acacius explained the likeness as one of will only, not extending to essence, and refused to be bound by his own defence of the Lucianic creed against Marcellus. Semiarian horror was not diminished when an extract was read from an obscene sermon preached by Eudoxius at Antioch. At last Eleusius broke in upon Acacius—'Any hole-and-corner doings of yours at Sirmium are no concern of ours. Your creed is not the Lucianic, and that is quite enough to condemn it.' This was decisive. Next morning the Semiarians had the church to themselves, for the Homœans, and even Leonas, refused to come. 'They might go and chatter in the church if they pleased.' So they deposed Acacius, Eudoxius, George of Alexandria, and six others.

The exiled patriarch of Alexandria was watching

from his refuge in the desert, and this was the time he chose for an overture of friendship to his old conservative enemies. If he was slow to see his opportunity, at least he used it nobly. The Eastern church has no more honoured name than that of Athanasius, yet even Athanasius rises above himself in his *De Synodis*. He had been a champion of controversy since his youth, and spent his manhood in the forefront of its hottest battle. The care of many churches rested on him, the pertinacity of many enemies wore out his life. Twice he had been driven to the ends of the earth, and twice come back in triumph; and now, far on in life, he saw his work again destroyed, himself once more a fugitive. We do not look for calm impartiality in a Demosthenes, and cannot wonder if the bitterness of his long exile grows on even Athanasius. Yet no sooner is he cheered with the news of hope, than the jealousies which had grown for forty years are hushed in a moment, as though the Lord himself had spoken peace to the tumult of the grey old exile's troubled soul. To the impenitent Arians he is as severe as ever, but for old enemies returning to a better mind he has nothing but brotherly consideration and respectful sympathy. Men like Basil of Ancyra, says he, are not to be set down as Arians or treated as enemies, but to be reasoned with as brethren who differ from us only about the use of a word which sums up their own teaching as well as ours. When they confess that the Lord is a true Son of God and not a creature, they grant all that we care to contend for. Their own *of like essence* without the addition of *from the essence* does not exclude the idea of a creature, but

<small>Athanasius *de Synodis*.</small>

THE VICTORY OF ARIANISM. 99

the two together are precisely equivalent to *of one essence*. Our brethren accept the two separately: we join them in a single word. Their *of like essence* is by itself misleading, for likeness is of properties and qualities, not of essence, which must be either the same or different. Thus the word rather suggests than excludes the limited idea of a sonship which means no more than a share of grace, whereas our *of one essence* quite excludes it. Sooner or later they will see their way to accept a term which is a necessary safeguard for the belief they hold in common with ourselves.

There could be no doubt of the opinion of the churches when the councils had both so decidedly refused the dated creed; but the court was not yet at the end of its resources. The Western deputies were sent back to Ariminum, and the bishops, already reduced to great distress by their long detention, were plied with threats and cajolery till most of them yielded. When Phœbadius and a score of others remained firm, their resistance was overcome by as shameless a piece of villany as can be found in history. Valens came forward and declared that he was not one of the Arians, but heartily detested their blasphemies. The creed would do very well as it stood, and the Easterns had accepted it already; but if Phœbadius was not satisfied, he was welcome to propose additions. A stringent series of anathemas was therefore drawn up against Arius and all his misbelief. Valens himself contributed one against 'those who say that the Son of God is a creature like other creatures.' The court party accepted everything, and the council

End of the Council of Ariminum.

met for a final reading of the amended creed. Shout after shout of joy rang through the church when Valens protested that the heresies were none of his, and with his own lips pronounced the whole series of anathemas; and when Claudius of Picenum produced a few more rumours of heresy, 'which my lord and brother Valens has forgotten,' they were disavowed with equal readiness. The hearts of all men melted towards the old dissembler, and the bishops dispersed from Ariminum in the full belief that the council would take its place in history among the bulwarks of the faith.

The Western council was dissolved in seeming harmony, but a strong minority disputed the conclusions of the Easterns at Seleucia. Both parties, therefore, hurried to Constantinople. But there Acacius was in his element. He held a splendid position as the bishop of a venerated church, the disciple and successor of Eusebius, and himself a patron of learning and a writer of high repute. His fine gifts of subtle thought and ready energy, his commanding influence and skilful policy, marked him out for a glorious work in history, and nothing but his own falseness degraded him to be the greatest living master of backstairs intrigue. If Athanasius is the Demosthenes of the Nicene age, Acacius will be its Æschines. He had found his account in abandoning conservatism for pure Arianism, and was now preparing to complete his victory by a new treachery to the Anomœans. He had anathematized *unlike* at Seleucia, and now sacrificed Aetius to the Emperor's dislike of him. After this it became possible to enforce the prohibition of the Nicene *of like essence*.

Conferences at Constantinople

THE VICTORY OF ARIANISM. 101

Meanwhile the final report arrived from Ariminum. Valens at once gave an Arian meaning to the anathemas of Phœbadius 'Not a creature like other creatures.' Then creature he is. 'Not from nothing.' Quite so: from the will of the Father. 'Eternal.' Of course, as regards the future. However, the Homœans repeated the process of swearing that they were not Arians; the Emperor threatened; and at last the Seleucian deputies signed the decisions of Ariminum late on the last night of the year 359.

Acacius had won his victory, and had now to pass sentence on his rivals. Next month a council was held at Constantinople. As the Semiarians of Asia were prudent enough to absent themselves, the Homœans were dominant. Its first step was to re-issue the creed of Nicé with a number of verbal changes. The anathemas of Phœbadius having served their purpose, were of course omitted. Next Aetius was degraded and anathematized for his impious and heretical writings, and as 'the author of all the scandals, troubles, and divisions.' This was needed to satisfy Constantius; but as many as nine bishops were found to protest against it. They were given six months to reconsider the matter, and soon began to form communities of their own. Having cleared themselves from the charge of heresy by laying the foundation of a permanent schism, the Homœans could proceed to the expulsion of the Semiarian leaders. As men who had signed the creed of Nicé could not well be accused of heresy, they were deposed for various irregularities.

Deposition of the Semiarians.

The Homœan supremacy established at Constantinople was limited to the East. Violence was its only resource beyond the Alps; and violence was out of the question after the mutiny at Paris (Jan. 360) had made Julian master of Gaul. Now that he could act for himself, common sense as well as inclination forbade him to go on with the mischievous policy of Constantius. So there was no further question of Arian domination. Few bishops were committed to the losing side, and those few soon disappeared in the course of nature. Auxentius the Cappadocian, who held the see of Milan till 374, must have been one of the last survivors of the victors of Ariminum. In the East, however, the Homœan supremacy lasted nearly twenty years. No doubt it was an artificial power, resting partly on court intrigue, partly on the divisions of its enemies; yet there was a reason for its long duration. Eusebian conservatism was fairly worn out, but the Nicene doctrine had not yet replaced it. Men were tired of these philosophical word-battles, and ready to ask whether the difference between Nicé and Nicæa was worth fighting about. The Homœan formula seemed reverent and safe, and its bitterest enemies could hardly call it false. When even the court preached peace and charity, the sermon was not likely to want an audience.

The Homœan supremacy.

The Homœans were at first less hostile to the Nicene faith than the Eusebians had been. After sacrificing Aetius and exiling the Semi-arians, they could hardly do without Nicene support. Thus their appointments were often made from the quieter men of Nicene leanings. If we have to set on the other side the enthronement of Eudoxius

The Homœan policy.

at Constantinople and the choice of Eunomius the Anomœan for the see of Cyzicus, we can only say that the Homœan party was composed of very discordant elements.

The most important nomination ascribed to Acacius is that of Meletius at Antioch to replace Eudoxius.

Appointment of Meletius. The new bishop was a man of distinguished eloquence and undoubted piety, and further suited for a dangerous elevation by his peaceful temper and winning manners. He was counted among the Homœans, and they had placed him a year before in the room of Eustathius at Sebastia, so that his uncanonical translation to Antioch engaged him all the more to remain on friendly terms with them. Such a man—and of course Acacius was shrewd enough to see it—would have been a tower of strength to them. Unfortunately, for once Acacius was not all-powerful. Some evil-disposed person put Constantius on demanding from the new bishop a sermon on the crucial text 'The Lord created me.'[1] Acacius, who preached first, evaded the test, but Meletius, as a man of honour, could not refuse to declare himself. To the delight of the congregation, his doctrine proved decidedly Nicene. It was a test for his hearers as well as for himself. He carefully avoided technical terms, repudiated Marcellus, and repeatedly deprecated controversy on the ineffable mystery of the divine generation. In a word, he followed closely the lines of the Sirmian creed; and his treatment by the Homœans is a decisive proof of their insincerity. The people applauded, but the courtiers were covered with shame. There was nothing for it

[1] Prov. viii. 21, LXX translation.

but to exile Meletius at once and appoint a new bishop. This time they made sure of their man by choosing Euzoius, the old friend of Arius. But the mischief was already done. The old congregation of Leontius was broken up, and a new schism, more dangerous than the Eustathian, formed round Meletius. Many jealousies still divided him from the Nicenes, but his bold confession was the first effective blow at the Homœan supremacy.

The idea of conciliating Nicene support was not entirely given up. Acacius remained on friendly terms with Meletius, and was still able to name Pelagius for the see of Laodicea. But Euzoius was an avowed Arian; Eudoxius differed little from him, and only the remaining scruples of Constantius delayed the victory of the Anomœans.

<small>Affairs in 361.</small>

CHAPTER VI.

THE REIGN OF JULIAN.

FLAVIUS CLAUDIUS JULIANUS was the son of Constantine's half-brother, Julius Constantius, by his second
<small>Earlier life of Julian.</small> wife, Basilina, a lady of the great Anician family. He was born in 331, and lost his mother a few months later, while his father and other relations perished in the massacre which followed Constantine's death. Julian and his half-brother Gallus escaped the slaughter to be kept almost as prisoners of state, surrounded through their youth with spies and taught by hypocrites a repulsive Christianity. Julian, however, had a literary education from his mother's old teacher, the eunuch Mardonius; and this was his happiness till he was old enough to attend the rhetoricians at Nicomedia and elsewhere. Gallus was for a while Cæsar in Syria (351–354), and after his execution, Julian's own life was only saved by the Empress Eusebia, who got permission for him to retire to the schools of Athens. In 355 he was made Cæsar in Gaul, and with much labour freed the province from the Germans. Early in 360 the soldiers mutinied at Paris and proclaimed Julian Augustus. Negotia-

tions followed, and it was not till the summer of 361 that Julian pushed down the Danube. By the time he halted at Naissus, he was master of three-quarters of the Empire. There seemed no escape from civil war now that the main army of Constantius was coming up from Syria. But one day two barbarian counts rode into Julian's camp with the news that Constantius was dead. A sudden fever had carried him off in Cilicia (Nov. 3, 361), and the Eastern army presented its allegiance to Julian Augustus.

Before we can understand Julian's influence on the Arian controversy, we shall have to take a wider view of the Emperor himself and of his policy towards the Christians generally. The life of Julian is one of the noblest wrecks in history. The years of painful self-repression and forced dissimulation which turned his bright youth to bitterness and filled his mind with angry prejudice, had only consolidated his self-reliant pride and firm determination to walk worthily before the gods. In four years his splendid energy and unaffected kindliness had won all hearts in Gaul; and Julian relaxed nothing of his sense of duty to the Empire when he found himself master of the world at the age of thirty.

Julian's heathenism

But here came in that fatal heathen prejudice, which put him in a false relation to all the living powers of his time, and led directly even to his military disaster in Assyria. Heathen pride came to him with Basilina's Roman blood, and the dream-world of his lonely youth was a world of heathen literature. Christianity was nothing to him but 'the slavery of a Persian prison.' Fine preachers of the kingdom of heaven were those fawning eunuchs and episcopal sycophants, with Constantius behind them, the murderer of all his family! Every force about him worked for heathenism. The teaching of Mardonius was practically heathen, and the rest were as heathen as utter worldliness could make them. He could see through men like George the pork-contractor or the shameless renegade Hecebolius. Full of thoughts like these, which corroded his mind the more for the danger of expressing them, Julian was easily won to heathenism by the fatherly welcome of the philosophers at Nicomedia (351). Like a voice of love from heaven came their teaching, and Julian gave himself heart and soul to the mysterious fascination of their lying theurgy. Henceforth King Sun was his guardian deity, and Greece his Holy Land, and the philosopher's mantle dearer to him than the diadem of empire. For ten more years of painful dissimulation Julian 'walked with the gods' in secret, before the young lion of heathenism could openly throw off the 'donkey's skin' of Christianity.

Once master of the world, Julian could see its needs without using the eyes of the Asiatic camarilla. First of all, Christian domination must be put down. Not that he wanted to raise a savage persecution. Cruelty had been well tried before, and it would be a poor success to stamp out the 'Galilean' imposture without putting something better in its place. As the Christians 'had filled the world with their tombs' (Julian's word for churches), so must it be filled with the knowledge of the living gods. Sacrifices were encouraged and a pagan hierarchy set up to oppose the Christian. Heathen schools

Julian's reorganisation of heathenism.

were to confront the Christian, and heathen almshouses were to grow up round them. Above all, the priests were to cultivate temperance and hospitality, and to devote themselves to grave and pious studies. Julian himself was a model of heathen purity, and spared no pains to infect his wondering subjects with his own enthusiasm for the cause of the immortal gods. Not a temple missed its visit, not a high place near his line of march was left unclimbed. As for his sacrifices, they were by the hecatomb. The very abjects called him Slaughterer.

Never was a completer failure. Crowds of course applauded Cæsar, but only with the empty cheers they gave the jockeys or the preachers. Multitudes came to see an Emperor's devotions, but they only quizzed his shaggy beard or tittered at the antiquated ceremonies. Sacrificial dinners kept the soldiers devout, and lavish bribery secured a good number of renegades—mostly waverers, who really had not much to change. Of the bishops, Pegasius of Ilium alone laid down his office for a priesthood; but he had always been a heathen at heart, and worshipped the gods even while he held his bishopric. The Christians upon the whole stood firm. Even the heathens were little moved. Julian's own teachers held cautiously aloof from his reforms; and if meaner men paused in their giddy round of pleasure, it was only to amuse themselves with the strange spectacle of imperial earnestness. Neither friends nor enemies seemed able to take him quite seriously.

His failure

Passing over scattered cases of persecution encouraged or allowed by Julian, we may state gene-

THE REIGN OF JULIAN.

rally that he aimed at degrading Christianity into a vulgar superstition, by breaking its connections with civilized government on one side, with liberal education on the other. One part of it was to deprive the 'Galileans' of state support and weed them out as far as might be from the public service, while still leaving them full freedom to quarrel amongst themselves; the other was to cut them off from literature by forbidding them to teach the classics. Homer and Hesiod were prophets of the gods, and must not be expounded by unbelievers. Matthew and Luke were good enough for barbarian ears like theirs. We need not pause to note the impolicy of an edict which Julian's own admirer Ammianus wishes 'buried in eternal silence.' Its effect on the Christians was very marked. Marius Victorinus, the favoured teacher of the Roman nobles, at once resigned his chair of rhetoric. The studies of his old age had brought him to confess his faith in Christ, and he would not now deny his Lord. Julian's own teacher Proæresius gave up his chair at Athens, refusing the special exemption which was offered him. It was not all loss for the Christians to be reminded that the gospel is revelation, not philosophy—life and not discussion. But Greek literature was far too weak to bear the burden of a sinking world, and its guardians could not have devised a more fatal plan than this of setting it in direct antagonism to the living power of Christianity. In our regret for the feud between Hellenic culture and the mediæval churches, we must not forget that it was Julian who drove in the wedge of separation.

Julian's policy against Christianity

We can now sum up in a sentence. Every blow struck at Christianity by Julian fell first on the Arianizers whom Constantius had left in power, and the reaction he provoked against heathen learning directly threatened the philosophical postulates of Arianism within the church. In both ways he powerfully helped the Nicene cause. The Homœans could not stand without court support, and the Anomœans threw away their rhetoric on men who were beginning to see how little ground is really common to the gospel and philosophy. Yet he cared little for the party quarrels of the Christians. Instead of condescending to take a side, he told them contemptuously to keep the peace. His first step was to proclaim full toleration for all sorts and sects of men. It was only too easy to strike at the church by doing common justice to the sects. A few days later came an edict recalling the exiled bishops. Their property was restored, but they were not replaced in their churches. Others were commonly in possession, and it was no business of Julian's to turn them out. The Galileans might look after their own squabbles. This sounds fairly well, and suits his professions of toleration; but Julian had a malicious hope of still further embroiling the ecclesiastical confusion. If the Christians were only left to themselves, they might be trusted 'to quarrel like beasts.'

Julian was gratified with a few unseemly wrangles, but the general result of his policy was unexpected. It took the Christians by surprise, and fairly shamed them into a sort of truce. The very divisions of churches are in some sense a sign of life, for men who do not care about religion will usually find something else to quarrel over. If nations redeem each other, so do parties; and the dignified slumber of a catholic uniformity may be more fatal to spiritual life than the vulgar wranglings of a thousand sects. The Christians closed their ranks before the common enemy. Nicenes and Arians forgot their enmity in the pleasant task of reviling the gods and cursing Julian. A yell of execration ran all along the Christian line, from the extreme Apollinarian right to the furthest Anomœan left. Basil of Cæsarea renounced the apostate's friendship; the rabble of Antioch assailed him with scurrilous lampoons and anti-pagan riots Nor were the Arians behind in hate. Blind old Maris of Chalcedon came and cursed him to his face. The heathens laughed, the Christians cursed, and Israel alone remembered Julian for good. 'Treasured in the house of Julianus Cæsar,' the vessels of the temple still await the day when Messiah-ben-Ephraim shall take them thence.

Back to their dioceses came the survivors of the exiled bishops, no longer travelling in pomp and circumstance to their noisy councils, but bound on the nobler errand of seeking out their lost or scattered flocks. Eusebius of Vercellæ and Lucifer left Upper Egypt, Marcellus and Basil returned to Ancyra, while Athanasius reappeared at Alexandria. The unfortunate George had led a wandering life since his expulsion in 358, and did not venture to leave the shelter of the court till late in 361. It was a rash move, for his flock had not forgotten him. Three days he spent in safety, but on the fourth came

Return of Athanasius, Feb 362

news that Constantius was dead and Julian master of the Empire. The heathen populace was wild with delight, and threw George straight into prison. Three weeks later they dragged him out and lynched him. Thus when Julian's edict came for the return of the exiles, Athanasius was doubly prepared to take advantage of it.

It was time to resume the interrupted work of the council of Seleucia. Semiarian violence frustrated Hilary's efforts, but Athanasius had things more in his favour, now that Julian had sobered Christian partizanship. If he wished the Galileans to quarrel, he also left them free to combine. So twenty-one bishops, mostly exiles, met at Alexandria in the summer of 362. Eusebius of Vercellæ was with Athanasius, but Lucifer had gone to Antioch, and only sent a couple of deacons to the meeting.

Council of Alexandria discusses

Four subjects claimed the council's attention. The first was the reception of Arians who came over to the Nicene side. The stricter party was for treating all opponents without distinction as apostates. Athanasius, however, urged a milder course. It was agreed that all comers were to be gladly received on the single condition of accepting the Nicene faith. None but the chiefs and active defenders of Arianism were even to be deprived of any ecclesiastical rank which they might be holding.

(1) Returning Arians.

A second subject of debate was the Arian doctrine of the Lord's humanity, which limited it to a human body. In opposition to this, the council declared that the Lord assumed also a human soul. In this they may have had in view,

(2) The Lord's human nature

THE REIGN OF JULIAN.

besides Arianism, the new theory of Apollinarius of Laodicea, which we shall have to explain presently.

The third subject before the council was an old misunderstanding about the term *hypostasis*. It had

(3) The words *person* and *essence*

been used in the Nicene anathemas as equivalent to *ousia* or *essence;* and so Athanasius used it still, to denote the common deity of all the persons of the Trinity. So also the Latins understood it, as the etymological representative of *substantia*, which was their translation (a very bad one by the way) of *ousia* (*essence*). Thus Athanasius and the Latins spoke of one *hypostasis* (*essence*) only. Meantime the Easterns in general had adopted Origen's limitation of it to the deity of the several *persons* of the Trinity in contrast with each other. Thus they meant by it what the Latins called *persona*,[1] and rightly spoke of three *hypostases* (*persons*). In this way East and West were at cross-purposes. The Latins, who spoke of one *hypostasis* (*essence*), regarded the Eastern three *hypostases* as tritheist; while the Greeks, who confessed three *hypostases* (*persons*), looked on the Western one *hypostasis* as Sabellian. As Athanasius had connections with both parties, he was a natural mediator. As soon as both views were stated before the council, both were seen to be orthodox. 'One *hypostasis*' (*essence*) was not Sabellian, neither was 'three *hypostases*' (*persons*) Arian. The decision was that each party might keep its own usage.

Affairs at Antioch remained for discussion. Now that Meletius was free to return, some decision had to

---

[1] *Persona*, again, was a legal term, not exactly corresponding to its Greek representative.

be made. The Eustathians had been faithful through thirty years of trouble, and Athanasius was specially bound to his old friends; yet, on the other hand, some recognition was due to the honourable confession of Meletius. As the Eustathians had no bishop, the simplest course was for them to accept Meletius. This was the desire of the council, and it might have been carried out if Lucifer had not taken advantage of his stay at Antioch to denounce Meletius as an associate of Arians. By way of making the division permanent, he consecrated the presbyter Paulinus as bishop for the Eustathians. When the mischief was done it could not be undone. Paulinus added his signature to the decisions of Alexandria, but Meletius was thrown back on his old connection with Acacius. Henceforth the rising Nicene party of Pontus and Asia was divided from the older Nicenes of Egypt and Rome by this unfortunate personal question.

(4) The schism at Antioch

Julian could not but see that Athanasius was master in Egypt. He may not have cared about the council, but the baptism of some heathen ladies at Alexandria roused his fiercest anger. He broke his rule of contemptuous toleration, and 'the detestable Athanasius' was an exile again before the summer was over. But his work remained. The leniency of the council was a great success, notwithstanding the calamity at Antioch. It gave offence, indeed, to zealots like Lucifer, and may have admitted more than one unworthy Arianizer. Yet its wisdom is evident. First one bishop, then another accepted the Nicene faith. Friendly Semiarians came in like

Fourth exile of Athanasius

Cyril of Jerusalem, old conservatives followed like Dianius of the Cappadocian Cæsarea, and at last the arch-heretic Acacius himself gave in his signature. Even the creeds of the churches were remodelled in a Nicene interest, as at Jerusalem and Antioch, in Cappadocia and Mesopotamia.

Nor were the other parties idle. The Homœan coalition was even more unstable than the Eusebian. Already before the death of Constantius there had been quarrels over the appointment of Meletius by one section of the party, of Eunomius by another. The deposition of Aetius was another bone of contention. Hence the coalition broke up of itself as soon as men were free to act. Acacius and his friends drew nearer to Meletius, while Eudoxius and Euzoius talked of annulling the condemnation of the Anomœan bishops at Constantinople. The Semiarians were busy too. Guided by Macedonius and Eleusius, the ejected bishops of Constantinople and Cyzicus, they gradually took up a middle position between Nicenes and Anomœans, confessing the Lord's deity with the one, and denying that of the Holy Spirit with the other. Like true Legitimists, who had learned nothing and forgotten nothing, they were satisfied to confirm the Seleucian decisions and re-issue their old Lucianic creed. Had they ceased to care for the Nicene alliance, or did they fancy the world had stood still since the Council of the Dedication?

The Arians under Julian.

Meanwhile the Persian war demanded Julian's attention. An emperor so full of heathen enthusiasm was not likely to forego the dreams of conquest which had brought so many of his predecessors on the path of glory in the East. His own part of the campaign was a splendid success. But when he had fought his way through the desert to the Tigris, he looked in vain for succours from the north. The Christians of Armenia would not fight for the apostate Emperor. Julian was obliged to retreat on Nisibis through a wasted country, and with the Persian cavalry hovering round. The campaign would have been at best a brilliant failure, but it was only converted into absolute disaster by the chance arrow (June 26, 363) which cut short his busy life. After all, he was only in his thirty-second year.

Julian's campaign in Persia (Mar. 5 to June 26, 363).

Christian charity will not delight in counting up the outbreaks of petty spite and childish vanity which disfigure a noble character of purity and self-devotion. Still less need we presume to speculate what Julian would have done if he had returned in triumph from the Persian war. His bitterness might have hardened into a renegade's malice, or it might have melted at our Master's touch. But apart from what he might have done, there is matter for the gravest blame in what he did. The scorner must not pass unchallenged to the banquet of the just. Yet when all is said against him, the clear fact remains that Julian lived a hero's life. Often as he was blinded by his impatience or hurried into injustice by his heathen prejudice, we cannot mistake a spirit of self-sacrifice and earnest piety as strange to worldling bishops as to the pleasure-loving heathen populace. Mysterious and full of tragic pathos is the irony of God in history, which allowed one of the very

Julian's character

noblest of the emperors to act the part of Jeroboam, and brought the old intriguer Maris of Chalcedon to cry against the altar like the man of God from Judah. But Maris was right, for Julian was the blinder of the two.

CHAPTER VII.

THE RESTORED HOMŒAN SUPREMACY.

JULIAN'S reign seems at first sight no more than a sudden storm which clears up and leaves everything much as it was before. Far from restoring heathenism, he could not even seriously shake the power of Christianity. No sooner was he dead than the philosophers disappeared, the renegades did penance, and even the reptiles of the palace came back to their accustomed haunts. Yet Julian's work was not in vain, for it tested both heathenism and Christianity. All that Constantine had given to the churches Julian could take away, but the living power of faith was not at Cæsar's beck and call. Heathenism was strong in its associations with Greek philosophy and culture, with Roman law and social life, but as a moral force among the common people, its weakness was contemptible. It could sway the wavering multitude with superstitious fancies, and cast a subtler spell upon the noblest Christian teachers, but its own adherents it could hardly lift above their petty quest of pleasure. Julian called aloud, and called in vain. A mocking echo was the only answer from that valley

Effects of Julian's reign

The Restored Homœan Supremacy. 119

of dry bones. Christianity, on the other side, had won the victory almost without a blow. Instead of ever coming to grapple with its mighty rival, the great catholic church of heathenism hardly reached the stage of apish mimicry. When its great army turned out to be a crowd of camp-followers, the alarm of battle died away in peals of defiant laughter. Yet the alarm was real, and its teachings were not forgotten. It broke up the revels of party strife, and partly roused the churches to the dangers of a purely heathen education. Above all, the approach of danger was a sharp reminder that our life is not of this world. They stood the test fairly well. Renegades or fanatics were old scandals, and signs were not wanting that the touch of persecution would wake the old heroic spirit which had fought the Empire from the catacombs and overcome it.

As Julian was the last survivor of the house of Constantine, his lieutenants were free to choose the worthiest of their comrades. But while his four barbarian generals were debating, one or two voices suddenly hailed Jovian as Emperor. The cry was taken up, and in a few moments the young officer found himself the successor of Augustus.

Jovian Emperor (June 27, 363)

Jovian was a brilliant colonel of the guards. In all the army there was not a goodlier person than he. Julian's purple was too small for his gigantic limbs. But that stately form was animated by a spirit of cowardly selfishness. Instead of pushing on with Julian's brave retreat, he saved the relics of his army by a disgraceful peace. Jovian was also a decided Christian, though his morals suited neither the purity of the gospel nor the dignity of his

Jovian's toleration.

imperial position. Even the heathen soldiers condemned his low amours and vulgar tippling. The faith he professed was the Nicene, but Constantine himself was less tolerant than Jovian. In this respect he is blameless. If Athanasius was graciously received at Antioch, even the Arians were told with scant ceremony that they might hold their assemblies as they pleased at Alexandria.

About this time the Anomœans organised their schism. Nearly four years had been spent in uncertain negotiations for the restoration of Aetius. The Anomœans counted on Eudoxius, but did not find him very zealous in the matter. At last, in Jovian's time, they made up their minds to set him at defiance by consecrating Pœmenius to the see of Constantinople. Other appointments were made at the same time, and Theophilus the Indian, who had a name for missionary work in the far East, was sent to Antioch to win over Euzoius. From this time the Anomœans were an organized sect.

The Anomœans form a sect.

But the most important document of Jovian's reign is the acceptance of the Nicene creed by Acacius of Cæsarea, with Meletius of Antioch and more than twenty others of his friends. Acacius was only returning to his master's steps when he explained *one in essence* by *like in essence*, and laid stress on the care with which 'the Fathers' had guarded its meaning. We may hope that Acacius had found out his belief at last. Still the connexion helped to widen the breach between Meletius and the older Nicenes.

Nicene successes

All these movements came to an end at the sudden death of Jovian (Feb. 16, 364.) The Pannonian Valentinian was chosen to succeed him, and a month later assigned the East to his brother Valens, reserving to himself the more important Western provinces. This was a lasting division of the Empire, for East and West were never again united for any length of time. Valentinian belongs to the better class of emperors. He was a soldier like Jovian, and, held much the same rank at his election. He was a decided Christian like Jovian, and, like him, free from the stain of persecution. Jovian's rough good-humour was replaced in Valentinian by a violent and sometimes cruel temper, but he had a sense of duty and was free from Jovian's vices. His reign was a laborious and honourable struggle with the enemies of the republic on the Rhine and the Danube. An uncultivated man himself, he still could honour learning, and in religion his policy was one of comprehensive toleration. If he refused to displace the few Arians whom he found in possession of Western sees like Auxentius at Milan, he left the churches free to choose Nicene successors. Under his wise rule the West soon recovered from the strife Constantius had introduced.

Valentinian Emperor

Valens was a weaker character, timid, suspicious, and slow, yet not ungentle in private life. He was as uncultivated as his brother, but not inferior to him in scrupulous care for his subjects. Only as Valens was no soldier, he preferred remitting taxation to fighting at the head of the legions. In both ways he is entitled to head the series of financial rather than unwarlike sovereigns whose cautious policy brought the Eastern Empire safely through the great barbarian invasions of the fifth century.

Character of Valens

The contest entered on a new stage in the reign of Valens. The friendly league of church and state at Nicæa had become a struggle for supremacy. Constantius endeavoured to dictate the faith of Christendom according to the pleasure of his eunuchs, while Athanasius reigned in Egypt almost like a rival for the Empire. And if Julian's reign had sobered party spirit, it had also shown that an emperor could sit again in Satan's seat. Valens had an obedient Homœan clergy, but no trappings of official splendour could enable Eudoxius or Demophilus to rival the imposing personality of Athanasius or Basil. Thus the Empire lost the moral support it looked for, and the church became embittered with its wrongs.

Breach between church and state

The breach involved a deeper evil. The ancient world of heathenism was near its dissolution. Vice and war, and latterly taxation, had dried up the springs of prosperity, and even of population, till Rome was perishing for lack of men. Cities had dwindled into villages, and of villages the very names had often disappeared. The stout Italian yeomen had been replaced by gangs of slaves, and these again by thinly scattered barbarian serfs. And if Rome grew weaker every day, her power for oppression seemed only to increase. Her fiscal system filled the provinces with ruined men. The Alps, the Taurus, and the Balkan swarmed with outlaws. But in the East men looked for refuge to the desert, where many a legend told of a people of brethren dwelling together in unity and serving God in peace beyond the reach of the officials. This was the time when the ascetic

Rise of monasticism.

spirit, which had long been hovering round the outskirts of Christianity, began to assume the form of monasticism. There were monks in Egypt—monks of Serapis—before Christianity existed, and there may have been Christian monks by the end of the third century. In any case, they make little show in history before the reign of Valens. Paul of Thebes, Hilarion of Gaza, and even the great Antony are only characters in the novels of the day. Now, however, there was in the East a real movement towards monasticism. All parties favoured it. The Semiarians were busy inside Mount Taurus; and though Acacians and Anomœans held more aloof, they could not escape an influence which even Julian felt. But the Nicene party was the home of the ascetics. In an age of indecision and frivolity like the Nicene, the most earnest striving after Christian purity will often degenerate into its ascetic caricature. Through the selfish cowardice of the monastic life we often see the loving sympathy of Christian self-denial. Thus there was an element of true Christian zeal in the enthusiasm of the Eastern Churches; and thus it was that the rising spirit of asceticism naturally attached itself to the Nicene faith as the strongest moral power in Christendom. It was a protest against the whole framework of society in that age, and therefore the alliance was cemented by a common enmity to the Arian Empire. It helped much to conquer Arianism, but it left a lasting evil in the lowering of the Christian standard. Henceforth the victory of faith was not to overcome the world, but to flee from it. Even heathen immorality was hardly more ruinous than the unclean ascetic spirit which defames God's holy ordinance as a form of sin which a too indulgent Lord will overlook.

Valens was only a catechumen, and had no policy to declare for the present. Events therefore continued to develop naturally. The Homœan bishops retained their sees, but their influence was fast declining. The Anomœans were forming a schism on one side, the Nicenes recovering power on the other. Unwilling signatures to the Homœan creed were revoked in all directions. Some even of its authors declared for Arianism with Euzoius, while others drew nearer to the Nicene faith like Acacius. On all sides the simpler doctrines were driving out the compromises. It was time for the Semiarians to bestir themselves if they meant to remain a majority in the East. The Nicenes seemed daily to gain ground. Lucifer had compromised them in one direction, Apollinarius in another, and even Marcellus had never been frankly disavowed; yet the Nicene cause advanced. A new question, however, was beginning to come forward. Hitherto the dispute had been on the person of the Lord, while that of the Holy Spirit was quite in the background. Significant as is the tone of Scripture, the proof is not on the surface. The divinity of the Holy Spirit is shown by many convergent lines of evidence, but it was still an open question whether that divinity amounts to co-essential and co-equal deity. Thus Origen leans to some theory of subordination, while Hilary limits himself with the utmost caution to the words of Scripture. If neither of them lays down in so many words that the Holy Spirit is God, much less does

New questions in controversy

either of them class him with the creatures, like Eunomius. The difficulty was the same as with the person of the Lord, that while the Scriptural data clearly pointed to his deity, its admission involved the dilemma of either Sabellian confusion or polytheistic separation. Now, however, it was beginning to be seen that the theory of hypostatic distinctions must either be extended to the Holy Spirit or entirely abandoned. Athanasius took one course, the Anomœans the other, but the Semiarians endeavoured to draw a distinction between the Lord's deity and that of the Holy Spirit. In truth, the two are logically connected. Athanasius pointed this out in the letters of his exile to Serapion, and the council of Alexandria condemned 'those who say that the Holy Spirit is a creature and distinct from the essence of the Son.' But logical connection is one thing, formal enforcement another. Athanasius and Basil to the last refused to make it a condition of communion. If any one saw the error of his Arian ways, it was enough for him to confess the Nicene creed. Thus the question remained open for the present.

Thus the Semiarians were free to do what they could against the Homœans. Under the guidance of Eleusius of Cyzicus, they held a council at Lampsacus in the summer of 364. It sat two months, and reversed the acts of the Homœans at Constantinople four years before. Eudoxius was deposed (in name) and the Semiarian exiles restored to their sees. With regard to doctrine, they adopted the formula *like according to essence*, on the ground that while likeness was needed to exclude

Council of Lampsacus (364).

a Sabellian (they mean Nicene) confusion, its express extension to essence was needed against the Arians. Nor did they forget to re-issue the Lucianic creed for the acceptance of the churches. They also discussed without result the deity of the Holy Spirit. Eustathius of Sebastia for one was not prepared to commit himself either way. The decisions were then laid before Valens.

But Valens was already falling into bad hands. Now that Julian was dead, the courtiers were fast recovering their influence, and Eudoxius had already secured the Emperor's support. The deputies of Lampsacus were ordered to hold communion with the bishop of Constantinople, and exiled on their refusal.

The Homœan policy of Valens.

Looking back from our own time, we should say that it was not a promising course for Valens to support the Homœans. They had been in power before, and if they had not then been able to establish peace in the churches, they were not likely to succeed any better after their heavy losses in Julian's time. It is therefore the more important to see the Emperor's motives. No doubt personal influences must count for a good deal with a man like Valens, whose private attachments were so steady. Eudoxius was, after all, a man of experience and learning, whose mild prudence was the very help which Valens needed. The Empress Dominica was also a zealous Arian, so that the courtiers were Arians too. No wonder if their master was sincerely attached to the doctrines of his friends. But Valens was not strong enough to impose his own likings on the Empire. No merit raised him to the throne; no education or experience prepared him for the august dignity he reached so suddenly in middle life. Conscientious and irresolute, he could not even firmly control the officials He had not the magic of Constantine's name behind him, and was prevented by Valentinian's toleration from buying support with the spoils of the temples.

Under these circumstances, he could hardly do otherwise than support the Homœans. Heathenism had failed in Julian's hands, and an Anomœan course was out of the question. A Nicene policy might answer in the West, but it was not likely to find much support in the East outside Egypt. The only alternative was to favour the Semiarians; and even that was full of difficulties. After all, the Homœans were still the strongest party in 365. They were in possession of the churches and commanded much of the Asiatic influence, and had no enmity to contend with which was not quite as bitter against the other parties. They also had astute leaders, and a doctrine which still presented attractions to the quiet men who were tired of controversy. Upon the whole, the Homœan policy was the easiest for the moment.

In the spring of 365 an imperial rescript commanded the municipalities, under a heavy penalty, to drive out the bishops who had been exiled by Constantius and restored by Julian. Thereupon the populace of Alexandria declared that the law did not apply to Athanasius, because he had not been restored by Julian. A series of dangerous riots followed, which obliged the prefect Flavianus to refer the question back to Valens. Other bishops were

<small>The exiles exiled again.</small>

less fortunate. Meletius had to retire from Antioch, Eustathius from Sebastia.

The Semiarians looked to Valentinian for help. He had received them favourably the year before, and his intercession was not likely to be disregarded now. Eustathius of Sebastia was therefore sent to lay their case before the court of Milan. As, however, Valentinian had already started for Gaul, the deputation turned aside to Rome and offered to Liberius an acceptance of the Nicene creed signed by fifty-nine Semiarians, and purporting to come from the council of Lampsacus and other Asiatic synods. The message was well received at Rome, and in due time the envoys returned to Asia to report their doings before a council at Tyana.

<small>Semiarian embassy to Liberius.</small>

Meanwhile the plans of Valens were interrupted by the news that Constantinople had been seized by a pretender. Procopius was a relative of Julian who had retired into private life, but whom the jealousy of Valens had forced to become a pretender. For awhile the danger was pressing. Procopius had won over to his side some of the best legions of the Empire, while his connexion with the house of Constantine secured him the formidable services of the Goths. But the great generals kept their faith to Valens, and the usurper's power melted away before them. A decisive battle at Nacolia in Phrygia (May 366) once more seated Valens firmly on his throne.

<small>Revolt of Procopius, Sept. 365.</small>

Events could scarcely have fallen out better for Eudoxius and his friends. Valens was already on their side, and now his zeal was quickened by the

THE RESTORED HOMŒAN SUPREMACY. 129

mortal terror he had undergone, perhaps also by shame at the unworthy panic in which he had already allowed the exiles to return. In an age when the larger number of professing Christians were content to spend most of their lives as catechumens, it was a decided step for an Emperor to come forward and ask for baptism. This, however, was the step taken by Valens in the spring of 367, which finally committed him to the Homœan side. By it he undertook to resume the policy of Constantius, and to drive out false teachers at the dictation of Eudoxius.

Baptism of Valens by Eudoxius (367).

The Semiarians were in no condition to resist. Their district had been the seat of the revolt, and their disgrace at court was not lessened by the embassy to Rome. So divided also were they, that while one party assembled a synod at Tyana to welcome the return of the envoys, another met in Caria to ratify the Lucianic creed again. Unfortunately however for Eudoxius, Valens was entangled in a war with the Goths for three campaigns, and afterwards detained for another year in the Hellespontine district, so that he could not revisit the East till the summer of 371. Meanwhile there was not much to be done. Athanasius had been formally restored to his church during the Procopian panic by Brasidas the notary (February 366), and was too strong to be molested again. Meletius also and others had been allowed to return at the same time, and Valens was too busy to disturb them. Thus there was a sort of truce for the next few years. Of Syria we hear scarcely anything, and even in Pontus the strife must

Interval in the controversy (366–371)

have been abated by the famine of 368. The little we find to record seems to belong to the year 367. On one side, Eunomius the Anomœan was sent into exile, but soon recalled on the intercession of the old Arian Valens of Mursa. On the other, the Semiarians were not allowed to hold the great synod at Tarsus, which was intended to complete their reconciliation with the Western Nicenes. These years form the third great break in the Arian controversy, and were hardly less fruitful of results than the two former breaks under Constantius and Julian. Let us therefore glance at the condition of the churches.

The Homœan party was the last hope of Arianism within the Empire. The original doctrine of Arius had been decisively rejected at Nicæa; the Eusebian coalition was broken up by the Sirmian manifesto; and if the Homœan union also failed, the fall of Arianism could not be long delayed. Its weakness is shown by the rise of a new Nicene party in the most Arian province of the Empire. Cappadocia is an exception to the general rule that Christianity flourished best where cities were most numerous. The polished vice of Antioch or Corinth presented fewer obstacles than the rude ignorance of *pagi* or country villages. Now Cappadocia was chiefly a country district. The walls of Cæsarea lay in ruins since its capture by the Persians in the reign of Gallienus, and the other towns of the province were small and few. Yet Julian found it incorrigibly Christian, and we hear but little of heathenism from Basil. We cannot suppose that the Cappadocian boors were civilized enough to be out of the reach of

<small>New Nicene party in Cappadocia</small>

heathen influence. It seems rather that the *paganismus* of the West was partly represented by Arianism. In Cappadocia the heresy found its first great literary champion in the sophist Asterius. Gregory and George were brought to Alexandria from Cappadocia, and afterwards Auxentius to Milan and Eudoxius to Constantinople. Philagrius also, the prefect who drove out Athanasius in 339, was another of their countrymen. Above all, the heresiarch Eunomius came from Cappadocia, and had abundance of admirers in his native district. In this old Arian stronghold the league was formed which decided the fate of Arianism. Earnest men like Meletius had only been attracted to the Homœans by their professions of reverence for the person of the Lord. When, therefore, it appeared that Eudoxius and his friends were no better than Arians after all, these men began to look back to the decisions of 'the great and holy council' of Nicæa. There, at any rate, they would find something independent of the eunuchs and cooks who ruled the palace. Of the old conservatives also, who were strong in Pontus, there were many who felt that the Semiarian position was unsound, and yet could find no satisfaction in the indefinite doctrine professed at court. Here then was one split in the Homœan, another in the conservative party. If only the two sets of malcontents could form a union with each other and with the older Nicenes of Egypt and the West, they would sooner or later be the arbiters of Christendom. If they could secure Valentinian's intercession, they might obtain religious freedom at once.

Such seems to have been the plan laid down by the man who was now succeeding Athanasius as leader of the Nicene party. Basil of Cæsarea was a disciple of the schools of Athens, and a master of heathen eloquence and learning. He was also man of the world enough to keep on friendly terms with men of all sorts. Amongst his friends we find Athanasius and Gregory of Nazianzus, Libanius the heathen rhetorician, the barbarian generals Arinthæus and Victor, the renegade Modestus, and the Arian bishop Euippius. He was a Christian also of a Christian family. His grandmother, Macrina, was one of those who fled to the woods in the time of Diocletian's persecution; and in after years young Basil learned from her the words of Gregory the Wonder worker. The connections of his early life were with the conservatives. He owed his baptism to Dianius of Cæsarea, and much encouragement in asceticism to Eustathius of Sebastia. In 359 he accompanied Basil of Ancyra from Seleucia to the conferences at Constantinople, and on his return home came forward as a resolute enemy of Arianism at Cæsarea. The young deacon was soon recognised as a power in Asia. He received the dying recantation of Dianius, and guided the choice of his successor Eusebius in 362. Yet he still acted with the Semiarians, and helped them with his counsel at Lampsacus. Indeed it was from the Semiarian side that he approached the Nicene faith. In his own city of Cæsarea Eusebius found him indispensable. When jealousies arose between them, and Basil withdrew to his rustic paradise in Pontus, he was recalled by the clamour of the people at the

THE RESTORED HOMŒAN SUPREMACY. 133

approach of Valens in 365. This time the danger was averted by the Procopian troubles, but henceforth Basil governed Eusebius, and the church of Cæsarea through him, till in the summer of 370 he succeeded to the bishopric himself.

The election was a critical one, for every one knew that a bishop like Basil would be a pillar of the
Basil bishop of Cæsarea Nicene cause. On one side were the officials and the lukewarm bishops, on the other the people and the better class of Semiarians. They had to make great efforts. Eusebius of Samosata came to Cæsarea to urge the wavering bishops, and old Gregory[1] was carried from Nazianzus on his litter to perform the consecration. There was none but Basil who could meet the coming danger. By the spring of 371 Valens had fairly started on his progress to the East. He travelled slowly through the famine-wasted provinces, and only reached Cæsarea in time for the great winter festival of Epiphany 372. The Nicene faith in Cappadocia was not the least of the abuses he was putting down. The bishops yielded in all directions, but Basil was unshaken. The rough threats of Modestus succeeded no better than the fatherly counsel of Euippius; and when Valens himself and Basil met face to face, the Emperor was overawed. More than once the order was prepared for the obstinate prelate's exile, but for one reason or another it was never issued. Valens went forward on his journey, leaving behind a princely gift for

[1] The father of Gregory of Nazianzus the Divine, who was bishop, as we shall see, of Sasima and Constantinople in succession, but never of Nazianzus.

Basil's poorhouse. He reached Antioch in April, and settled there for the rest of his reign, never again leaving Syria till the disasters of the Gothic war called him back to Europe.

Armed with spiritual power which in some sort extended from the Bosphorus to Armenia, Basil could now endeavour to carry out his plan. Homœan malcontents formed the nucleus of the league, but conservatives began to join it, and Athanasius gave his patriarchal blessing to the scheme. The difficulties, however, were very great. The league was full of jealousies. Athanasius indeed might frankly recognise the soundness of Meletius, though he was committed to Paulinus, but others were less liberal, and Lucifer of Calaris was forming a schism on the question. Some, again, were lukewarm in the cause and many sunk in worldliness, while others were easily diverted from their purpose. The sorest trial of all was the selfish coldness of the West. Basil might find here and there a kindred spirit like Ambrose of Milan after 374; but the confessors of 355 were mostly gathered to their rest, and the church of Rome paid no regard to sufferings which were not likely to reach herself.

Basil's difficulties.

Nor was Basil quite the man for such a task as this. His courage indeed was indomitable. He ruled Cappadocia from a sick-bed, and bore down opposition by sheer strength of his inflexible determination. The very pride with which his enemies reproached him was often no more than a strong man's consciousness of power; and to this unwearied energy he joined an ascetic fervour which secured the devotion of his friends, a knowledge of the world which often turned aside the fury of his enemies, and a flow of warm-hearted rhetoric which never failed to command the admiration of outsiders. Yet after all we miss the lofty self-respect which marks the later years of Athanasius. Basil was involved in constant difficulties by his own pride and suspicion. We cannot, for example, imagine Athanasius turning two presbyters out of doors as 'spies.' But the ascetic is usually too full of his own plans to feel sympathy with others, too much in earnest to feign it like a diplomatist. Basil had enough worldly prudence to keep in the background his belief in the Holy Spirit, but not enough to protect even his closest friends from the outbreaks of his imperious temper. Small wonder if the great scheme met with many difficulties.

A specimen or two may be given, from which it will be seen that the difficulties were not all of Basil's making. When Valens divided Cappadocia in 372, the capital of the new province was fixed at Tyana. Thereupon Bishop Anthimus argued that ecclesiastical arrangements necessarily follow civil, and claimed the obedience of its bishops as due to him and not to Basil. Peace was patched up after an unseemly quarrel, and Basil disposed of any future claims from Anthimus by getting the new capital transferred to Podandus.

Disputes with (1) Anthimus

The dispute with Anthimus was little more than a personal quarrel, so that it was soon forgotten. The old Semiarian Eustathius of Sebastia was able to give more serious annoyance. He was a man too active to be ignored, too unstable to be

(2) Eustathius

trusted, too famous for ascetic piety to be lightly made
an open enemy. His friendship was compromising,
his enmity dangerous. We left him professing the
Nicene faith before the council of Tyana. For the
next three years we lose sight of him. He reappears
as a friend of Basil in 370, and heartily supported
him in his strife with Valens. Eustathius was at any
rate no time-server. He was drawn to Basil by old
friendship and a common love of asceticism, but almost
equally repelled by the imperious orthodoxy of a stronger
will than his own. And Basil for a long time clung
to his old teacher, though the increasing distrust of
staunch Nicenes like Theodotus of Nicopolis was
beginning to attack himself. His peacemaking was
worse than a failure. First he offended Theodotus,
then he alienated Eustathius. The suspicious zeal of
Theodotus was quieted in course of time, but Eustathius
never forgave the urgency which wrung from him his
signature to a Nicene confession. He had long been
leaning the other way, and now he turned on Basil
with all the bitterness of broken friendship. To such
a man the elastic faith of the Homœans was a welcome
refuge. If they wasted little courtesy on their convert, they did not press him to strain his conscience by
signing what he ought not to have signed.

The Arian controversy was exhausted for the present,
and new questions were already beginning to take its
place. While Basil and Eustathius were
preparing the victory of asceticism in the
next generation, Apollinarius had already essayed the
christological problem of Ephesus and Chalcedon;
and Apollinarius was no common thinker. If his

efforts were premature, he at least struck out the most suggestive of the ancient heresies. Both in what he saw and in what he failed to see, his work is full of meaning for our own time. Apollinarius and his father were Christian literary men of Laodicea in Syria, and stood well to the front of controversy in Julian's days. When the rescript came out which forbade the Galileans to teach the classics, they promptly undertook to form a Christian literature by throwing Scripture into classical forms. The Old Testament was turned into Homeric verse, the New into Platonic dialogues. Here again Apollinarius was premature. There was indeed no reason why Christianity should not have as good a literature as heathenism, but it would have to be a growth of many ages. In doctrine Apollinarius was a staunch Nicene, and one of the chief allies of Athanasius in Syria. But he was a Nicene of an unusual type, for the side of Arianism which specially attracted his attention was its denial of the Lord's true manhood. It will be remembered that according to Arius the created Word assumed human flesh and nothing more. Eustathius of Antioch had long ago pointed out the error, and the Nicene council shut it out by adding *was made man* to the *was made flesh* of the Cæsarean creed. It was thus agreed that the lower element in the incarnation was man, not mere flesh; in other words, the Lord was perfect man as well as perfect God. But in that case, how can God and man form one person? In particular, the freedom of his human will is inconsistent with the fixity of the divine. Without free-will he was not truly man; yet free-will always leads to sin. If all men are sinners, and the Lord was not a sinner, it seemed to follow that he was not true man like other men. Yet in that case the incarnation is a mere illusion. The difficulty was more than Athanasius himself could fully solve. All that he could do was to hold firmly the doctrine of the Lord's true manhood as declared by Scripture, and leave the question of his free-will for another age to answer.

The analysis of human nature which we find in Scripture is twofold. In many passages there is a moral division into the spirit and the flesh—all that draws us up towards heaven and all that draws us down to earth. It must be carefully noted (what ascetics of all ages have overlooked) that the flesh is not the body. Envy and hatred are just as much works of the flesh[1] as revelling and uncleanness. It is not the body which lusts against the soul, but the evil nature running through them both which refuses the leading of the Spirit of God. But these are practical statements: the proper psychology of Scripture is given in another series of passages. It comes out clearly in 1 Thess. v. 23—'your whole spirit, and soul, and body be preserved blameless unto the coming of our Lord Jesus Christ.' Here the division is threefold. The body we know pretty well, as far as concerns its material form. The soul however, is not the 'soul' of common language. It is only the seat of the animal life which we share with the beasts. Above the soul, beyond the ken of Aristotle, Scripture reveals the spirit as the seat of the immortal life which is to pass the gate of death

The Apollinarian system

[1] Gal. v. 19-21.

unharmed. Now it is one chief merit of Apollinarius (and herein he has the advantage over Athanasius) that he based his system on the true psychology of Scripture. He argued that sin reaches man through the will, whose seat is in the spirit. Choice for good or for evil is in the will. Hence Adam fell through the weakness of the spirit. Had that been stronger, he would have been able to resist temptation. So it is with the rest of us: we all sin through the weakness of the spirit. If then the Lord was a man in whom the mutable human spirit was replaced by the immutable Divine Word, there will be no difficulty in understanding how he could be free from sin. Apollinarius, however, rightly chose to state his theory the other way—that the Divine Word assumed a human body and a human soul, and himself took the place of a human spirit. So far we see no great advance on the Arian theory of the incarnation. If the Lord had no true human spirit, he is no more true man than if he had nothing human but the body. We get a better explanation of his sinlessness, but we still get it at the expense of his humanity. In one respect the Arians had the advantage. Their created Word is easier joined with human flesh than the Divine Word with a human body and a human soul. At this point, however, Apollinarius introduced a thought of deep significance—that the spirit in Christ was human spirit, although divine. If man was made in the image of God, the Divine Word is not foreign to that human spirit which is in his likenesss, but is rather the true perfection of its image. If, therefore, the Lord had the divine Word instead of the human spirit of other men, he is not the less human, but the more so for the difference. Furthermore, the Word which in Christ was human spirit was eternal. Apart then from the incarnation, the Word was archetypal man as well as God. Thus we reach the still more solemn thought that the incarnation is not a mere expedient to get rid of sin, but the historic revelation of what was latent in the Word from all eternity. Had man not sinned, the Word must still have come among us, albeit not through shame and death. It was his nature that he should come. If he was man from eternity, it was his nature to become in time like men on earth, and it is his nature to remain for ever man. And as the Word looked down on mankind, so mankind looked upward to the Word. The spirit in man is a frail and shadowy thing apart from Christ, and men are not true men till they have found in him their immutable and sovereign guide. Thus the Word and man do not confront each other as alien beings. They are joined together in their inmost nature, and (may we say it?) each receives completion from the other.

The system of Apollinarius is a mighty outline whose details we can hardly even now fill in; yet as a system it is certainly a failure. His own contemporaries may have done him something less than justice, but they could not follow his daring flights of thought when they saw plain errors in his teaching. After all, Apollinarius reaches no true incarnation. The Lord is something very like us, but he is not one of us. The spirit is surely an essential part of man, and without a true human spirit he could have no true human choice or growth or life; and

<small>Criticism of Apollinarianism.</small>

indeed Apollinarius could not allow him any. His work is curtailed also like his manhood, for (so Gregory of Nyssa put it) the spirit which the Lord did not assume is not redeemed. Apollinarius understood even better than Athanasius the kinship of true human nature to its Lord, and applied it with admirable skill to explain the incarnation as the expression of the eternal divine nature. But he did not see so well as Athanasius that sin is a mere intruder among men. It was not a hopeful age in which he lived. The world had gone a long way downhill since young Athanasius had sung his song of triumph over fallen heathenism. Roman vice and Syrian frivolity, Eastern asceticism and Western legalism, combined to preach, in spite of Christianity, that the sinfulness of mankind is essential. So instead of following out the pregnant hint of Athanasius that sin is no true part of human nature (else were God the author of evil), Apollinarius cut the knot by refusing the Son of Man a human spirit as a thing of necessity sinful. Too thoughtful to slur over the difficulty like Pelagius, he was yet too timid to realize the possibility of a conquest of sin by man, even though that man were Christ himself.

Apollinarius and his school contributed not a little to the doctrinal confusion of the East. His ideas were

The Apollinarians.

current for some time in various forms, and are attacked in some of the later works of Athanasius; but it was not till about 375 that they led to a definite schism, marked by the consecration of the presbyter Vitalis to the bishopric of Antioch. From this time, Apollinarian bishops disputed many of the Syrian sees with Nicenes and Anomœans. Their adherents were also scattered over Asia, and supplied one more element of discord to the noisy populace of Constantinople.

The declining years of Athanasius were spent in peace. Valens had restored him in good faith, and never afterwards molested him. If Lucius the Arian returned to Alexandria to try his chance as bishop, the officials gave him no connivance—nothing but sorely needed shelter from the fury of the mob. Arianism was nearly extinct in Egypt.

Last years of Athanasius (366–373)

One of his last public acts was to receive an embassy from Marcellus, who was still living in extreme old age at Ancyra. Some short time before 371, the deacon Eugenius presented to him a confession on behalf of the 'innumerable multitude' who still owned Marcellus for their father. 'We are not heretics, as we are slandered. We specially anathematize Arianism, confessing, like our fathers at Nicæa, that the Son is no creature, but of the essence of the Father and co-essential with the Father; and by the Son we mean no other than the Word. Next we anathematize Sabellius, for we confess the eternity and reality of the Son and the Holy Spirit. We anathematize also the Anomœans, in spite of their pretence not to be Arians. We anathematize finally the Arianizers who separate the Word from the Son, giving the latter a beginning at the incarnation because they do not confess him to be very God. Our own doctrine of the incarnation is that the Word did not come down as on the prophets, but truly became flesh and took a servant's form, and

Athanasius and Marcellus (before 371)

as regards flesh was born as a man.' There is no departure here from the original doctrine of Marcellus, for the eternity of the Son means nothing more than the eternity of the Word. The memorial, however, was successful. Though Athanasius was no Marcellian, he was as determined as ever to leave all questions open which the great council had forborne to close. The new Nicenes of Pontus, on the other hand, inherited the conservative dread of Marcellus, so that it was a sore trial to Basil when Athanasius refused to sacrifice the old companion of his exile. Even the great Alexandrian's comprehensive charity is hardly nobler than his faithfulness to erring friends. Meaner men might cherish the petty jealousies of controversy, but the veterans of the great council once more recognised their fellowship in Christ. They were joined in life, and in death they were not divided.

Marcellus passed away in 371, and Athanasius two years later. The victory was not yet won, the goal of half a century was still beyond the sight of men; yet Athanasius had conquered Arianism. Of his greatness we need say no more. Some will murmur of 'fanaticism' before the only Christian whose grandeur awed the scoffer Gibbon So be it that his greatness was not unmixed with human passion; but those of us who have seen the light of heaven shining from some saintly face, or watched with kindling hearts and solemn thankfulness some mighty victory of Christian faith, will surely know that it was the spirit of another world which dwelt in Athanasius. To him more than any one we owe it that the question of Arianism did not lose itself in

Death of Athanasius (373).

personalities and quibbles, but took its proper place as a battle for the central message of the gospel, which is its chief distinction from philosophy and heathenism.

Instantly Alexandria was given up to the Arians, and Lucius repeated the outrages of Gregory and George. The friends of Athanasius were exiled, and his successor Peter fled to Rome. Meanwhile the school of Marcellus died away. In 375 his surviving followers addressed a new memorial to the Egyptian exiles at Sepphoris, in which they plainly confessed the eternal Sonship so long evaded by their master. Basil took no small offence when the exiles accepted the memorial. 'They were not the only zealous defenders of the Nicene faith in the East, and should not have acted without the consent of the Westerns and of their own bishop, Peter. In their haste to heal one schism they might cause another if they did not make it clear that the heretics had come over to them, and not they to the heretics.' This, however, was mere grumbling. Now that the Marcellians had given up the point in dispute, there was no great difficulty about their formal reconciliation. The West held out for Marcellus after his own disciples had forsaken him, so that he was not condemned at Rome till 380, nor by name till 381.

Meanwhile the churches of Asia seemed in a state of universal dissolution. Disorder under Constantius had become confusion worse confounded under Valens. The exiled bishops were so many centres of disaffection, and personal quarrels had full scope everywhere. Thus when Basil's brother Gregory was expelled from Nyssa by a riot got up by Anthimus of Tyana, he took refuge under the eyes of Anthimus at Doara, where a similar riot had driven out the Arian bishop. Pastoral work was carried on under the greatest difficulties. The exiles could not attend to their churches, the schemers would not, and the fever of controversy was steadily demoralizing both flocks and pastors.

Creeds were in the same confusion. The Homœans as a body had no consistent principle at all beyond the rejection of technical terms, so that their doctrinal statements are very miscellaneous.

(2) Creeds

They began with the indefinite Sirmian creed, but the confession they imposed on Eustathius of Sebastia was purely Macedonian. Some of their bishops were Nicenes, others Anomœans. There was room for all in the happy family presided over by Eudoxius and his successor Demophilus. In this anarchy of doctrine, the growth of irreligious carelessness kept pace with that of party bitterness. Ecclesiastical history records no clearer period of decline than this. There is a plain descent from Athanasius to Basil, a rapid one from Basil to Theophilus and Cyril. The victors of Constantinople are but the epigoni of a mighty contest.

Hopeful signs indeed were not entirely wanting. If the Nicene cause did not seem to gain much ground in Pontus, it was at least not losing. While Basil held the court in check, the rising power of asceticism was declaring itself every day more plainly on his side. One schism was healed by the reception of the Marcellians; and if Apollinarius

Hopeful signs

was forming another, he was at least a resolute enemy of Arianism. The submission of the Lycian bishops in 375 helped to isolate the Semiarian phalanx in Asia, and the Illyrian council held in the same year by Ambrose was the first effective help from the West. It secured a rescript of Valentinian in favour of the Nicenes; and if he did not long survive, his action was enough to show that Valens might not always be left to carry out his plans undisturbed.

CHAPTER VIII.

THE FALL OF ARIANISM.

THE fiftieth year from the great council came and went, and brought no relief to the calamities of the churches. Meletius and Cyril were still in exile, East and West were still divided over the consecration of Paulinus, and now even Alexandria had become the prey of Lucius. The leaden rule of Valens still weighed down the East, and Valens was scarcely yet past middle life, and might reign for many years longer. The deliverance came suddenly, and the Nicene faith won its victory in the confusion of the greatest disaster which had ever yet befallen Rome.

<small>Prospects in 375</small>

In the year 376 the Empire still seemed to stand unshaken within the limits of Augustus. If the legions had retired from the outlying provinces of Dacia and Carduene, they more than held their ground on the great river frontiers of the Euphrates, the Danube, and the Rhine. If Julian's death had seemed to let loose all the enemies of Rome at once, they had all been repulsed. While the Persian advance was checked by the obstinate patriotism of Armenia, Valens

<small>The Empire in 376</small>

reduced the Goths to submission, and his Western colleague drove the Germans out of Gaul and recovered Britain from the Picts. The Empire had fully held its own through twelve years of incessant warfare; and if there were serious indications of exhaustion in the dwindling of the legions and the increase of the barbarian auxiliaries, in the troops of brigands who infested every mountain district, in the alarming decrease of population, and above all in the ruin of the provinces by excessive taxation, it still seemed inconceivable that real danger could ever menace Rome's eternal throne.

But while the imperial statesmen were watching the Euphrates, the storm was gathering on the Danube. The Goths in Dacia had been learning husbandry and Christianity since Aurelian's time, and bade fair soon to become a civilized people. Heathenism was already half abandoned, and their nomad habits half laid aside. But when the Huns came up suddenly from the steppes of Asia, the stately Gothic warriors fled almost without a blow from the hordes of wild dwarfish horsemen. The Ostrogoths became the servants of their conquerors, and the heathens of Athanaric found a refuge in the recesses of the Transylvanian forests. But Fritigern was a Christian. Rome had helped him once before, and Rome might help him now. A whole nation of panic-stricken warriors crowded to the banks of the Danube. There was but one inviolable refuge in the world, and that was beneath the shelter of the Roman eagles. Only let them have some of the waste lands in Thrace, and they would be glad to do the Empire faithful ser-

THE FALL OF ARIANISM. 149

vice. When conditions had been settled, the Goths were brought across the river. Once on Roman ground, they were left to the mercy of officials whose only thought was to make the famished barbarians a prey to their own rapacity and lust. Before long the Goths broke loose and spread over the country, destroying whatever cultivation had survived the desolating misgovernment of the Empire. Outlaws and deserters were willing guides, and crowds of fresh barbarians came in to share the spoil. The Roman generals found it no easy task to keep the field.

First the victories of Claudius and Aurelian, and then the statesmanship of Constantine, had stayed for a century the tide of Northern war, but now the Empire was again reduced to fight for its existence. Its rulers seemed to understand the crisis. The East was drained of all available troops, and Sebastian the Manichee, the old enemy of Athanasius, was placed in command. Gratian hurried Thraceward with the Gaulish legions, and at last Valens thought it time to leave his pleasant home at Antioch for the field of war. Evil omens beset his march, but no omen could be worse than his own impulsive rashness. With a little prudence, such a force as he had gathered round the walls of Hadrianople was an overmatch for any hordes of barbarians. But Valens determined to storm the Gothic camp without waiting for his Western colleague. Rugged ground and tracts of burning grass delayed his march, so that it was long past noon before he neared the line of waggons, later still before the Gothic trumpet sounded. But the Roman army was in hopeless rout at sundown. The

Battle of Hadrianople (Aug 9, 378)

Goths came down 'like a thunderbolt on the mountain tops,' and all was lost. Far into the night the slaughtering went on. Sebastian fell, the Emperor was never heard of more, and full two-thirds of the Roman army perished in a scene of unequalled horror since the butchery of Cannæ.

Beneath that crushing blow the everlasting Empire shook from end to end. The whole power of the East had been mustered with a painful effort to the struggle, and the whole power of the East had been shattered in a summer's day. For the first time since the days of Gallienus, the Empire could place no army in the field. But Claudius and Aurelian had not fought in vain, nor were the hundred years of respite lost. If the dominion of Western Europe was transferred for ever to the Northern nations, the walls of Constantinople had risen to bar their eastward march, and Christianity had shown its power to awe their boldest spirits. The Empire of the Christian East withstood the shock of Hadrianople—only the heathen West sank under it. When once the old barriers of civilization on the Danube and the Rhine were broken through, the barbarians poured in for centuries like a flood of mighty waters overflowing. Not till the Northman and the Magyar had found their limit at the siege of Paris and the battle of the Lechfeld could Europe feel secure. The Roman Empire and the Christian Church alone rode out the storm which overthrew the ancient world. But the Christian Church was founded on the ever-living Rock, the Roman Empire rooted deep in history. Arianism was a thing of yesterday and had no principle of life, and therefore it vanished in the crash of Hadrianople. The Homœan supremacy had come to rest almost wholly on imperial misbelief. The mob of the capital might be in its favour, and the virtues of isolated bishops might secure it some support elsewhere; but serious men were mostly Nicenes or Anomœans. Demophilus of Constantinople headed the party, and his blunders did it almost as much harm as the profane jests of Eudoxius. At Antioch Euzoius, the last of the early Arians, was replaced by Dorotheus. Milan under Ambrose was aggressively Nicene, and the Arian tyrants were very weak at Alexandria. On the other hand, the greatest of the Nicenes had passed away, and few were left who could remember the great council's meeting. Athanasius and Hilary were dead, and even Basil did not live to greet an orthodox Emperor. Meletius of Antioch was in exile, and Cyril of Jerusalem and the venerated Eusebius of Samosata, while Gregory of Nazianzus had found in the Isaurian mountains a welcome refuge from his hated diocese of Sasima. If none of the living Nicenes could pretend to rival Athanasius, they at least outmatched the Arians.

As Valens left no children, the Empire rested for the moment in the hands of his nephew, Gratian, a youth of not yet twenty. Gratian, however, was wise enough to see that it was no time to cultivate religious quarrels. He, therefore, began by proclaiming toleration to all but Anomœans and Photinians. As toleration was still the theory of the Empire, and none but the Nicenes were practically molested, none but the Nicenes gained anything by

Gratian's toleration.

the edict. But mere toleration was all they needed. The exiled bishops found little difficulty in resuming the government of their flocks, and even in sending missions to Arian strongholds. The Semiarians were divided. Numbers went over to the Nicenes, while others took up an independent or Macedonian position. The Homœan power in the provinces fell of itself before it was touched by persecution. It scarcely even struggled against its fate. At Jerusalem indeed party spirit ran as high as ever, but Alexandria was given up to Peter almost without resistance. We find one or two outrages like the murder of Eusebius of Samosata by an Arian woman in a country town, who threw down a tile on his head, but we hardly ever find a Homœan bishop heartily supported by his flock.

Constantinople itself was now the chief stronghold of the Arians. They had held the churches since 340, and were steadily supported by the court. Thus the city populace was devoted to Arianism, and the Nicenes were a mere remnant, without either church or teacher. The time, however, was now come for a mission to the capital. Gregory of Nazianzus was the son of Bishop Gregory, born about the time of the Nicene council. His father was already presbyter of Nazianzus, and held the bishopric for nearly half a century. Young Gregory was a student of many schools. From the Cappadocian Cæsarea he went on to the Palestinian, and thence to Alexandria; but Athens was the goal of his student-life. Gregory and Basil and Prince Julian met at the feet of Proæresius. They all did credit to his eloquence, but there the likeness

Gregory of Nazianzus.

329–374.

THE FALL OF ARIANISM. 153

ends. Gregory disliked Julian's strange, excited manner, and persuaded himself in later years that he had even then foreseen the evil of the apostate's reign. With Basil, on the other hand his friendship was for life. They were well-matched in eloquence, in ascetic zeal, and in opposition to Arianism, though Basil's imperious ways were a trial to Gregory's gentler and less active spirit. During the quarrel with Anthimus of Tyana, Basil thought fit to secure the disputed possession of Sasima by making it a bishopric. It was a miserable post-station—'No water, no grass, nothing but dust and carts, and groans and howls, and small officials with their usual instruments of torture.' Gregory was made bishop of Sasima against his will, and never fairly entered on his repulsive duties. After a few years' retirement, he came forward to undertake the mission to Constantinople. The great city was a city of triflers. They jested at the actors and the preachers without respect of persons, and followed with equal eagerness the races and the theological disputes. Anomœans abounded in their noisy streets, and the graver Novatians and Macedonians were infected with the spirit of wrangling. Gregory's austere character and simple life were in themselves a severe rebuke to the lovers of pleasure round him. He began his work in a private house, and only built a church when the numbers of his flock increased. He called it his Anastasia,—the church of the resurrection of the faith. The mob was hostile—one night they broke into his church—but the fruit of his labours was a growing congregation of Nicenes in the capital.

372.

379

Gratian's next step was to share his burden with a colleague. If the care of the whole Empire had been too much for Diocletian or Valentinian, Gratian's were not the Atlantean shoulders which could bear its undivided weight. In the far West, at Cauca near Segovia, there lived a son of Theodosius, the recoverer of Britain and Africa, whose execution had so foully stained the opening of Gratian's reign. That memory of blood was still fresh, yet in that hour of overwhelming danger Gratian called young Theodosius to be his honoured colleague and deliverer. Early in 379 he gave him the conduct of the Gothic war. With it went the Empire of the East.

Theodosius Emperor in the East (379).

Theodosius was neither Greek nor Asiatic, but a stranger from the Spanish West, endued with a full measure of Spanish courage and intolerance. As a general he was the most brilliant Rome had seen since Julian's death. Men compared him to Trajan, and in a happier age he might have rivalled Trajan's fame. But now the Empire was ready to perish. The beaten army was hopelessly demoralized, and Theodosius had to form a new army of barbarian legionaries before the old tradition of Roman superiority could resume its wonted sway. It soon appeared that the Goths could do nothing with their victory, and sooner or later would have to make their peace with Rome. Theodosius drove them inland in the first campaign; and while he lay sick at Thessalonica in the second, Gratian or his generals received the submission of the Ostrogoths. Fritigern died the same year, and his old rival Athanaric was a fugitive before

End of the Gothic war

THE FALL OF ARIANISM. 155

it ended. When the returning Ostrogoths dislodged him from his Transylvanian forest, he was welcomed with honourable courtesy by Theodosius in person at Constantinople. But the old enemy of Rome and Christianity had only come to lay his bones on Roman soil. In another fortnight the barbarian chief was carried out with kingly splendour to his Roman funeral. Theodosius had nobly won Athanaric's inheritance. His wondering Goths at once took service with their conqueror: chief after chief submitted, and the work of peace was completed on the Danube in the autumn of 382.

We can now return to ecclesiastical affairs. The dangerous illness of Theodosius in 380 had important consequences, for his baptism by Ascholius of Thessalonica was the natural signal for a more decided policy. Ascholius was a zealous Nicene, so that Theodosius was committed to the Nicene side as effectually as Valens had been to the Homœan; and Theodosius was less afraid of strong measures than Valens. His first rescript (Feb. 27, 380) commands all men to follow the Nicene doctrine 'committed by the apostle Peter to the Romans, and now professed by Damasus of Rome and Peter of Alexandria,' and plainly threatens to impose temporal punishments on the heretics. Here it will be seen that Theodosius abandons Constantine's test of orthodoxy by subscription to a creed. It seemed easier now, and more in the spirit of Latin Christianity, to require communion with certain churches. The choice of Rome is natural, the addition of Alexandria shows that the Emperor was still a stranger to the mysteries of Eastern partizanship.

Baptism of Theodosius

There was no reason for delay when the worst dangers of the Gothic war were over. Theodosius made his formal entry into Constantinople, November 24, 380, and at once required the bishop either to accept the Nicene faith or to leave the city. Demophilus honourably refused to give up his heresy, and adjourned his services to the suburbs. So ended the forty years of Arian domination in Constantinople. But the mob was still Arian, and their stormy demonstrations when the cathedral of the Twelve Apostles was given up to Gregory of Nazianzus were enough to make Theodosius waver. Arian influence was still strong at court, and Arian bishops came flocking to Constantinople. Low as they had fallen, they could still count among them the great name of Ulfilas. But he could give them little help, for though the Goths of Mœsia were faithful to the Empire, Theodosius preferred the stalwart heathens of Athanaric to their Arian countrymen. Ulfilas died at Constantinople like Athanaric, but there was no royal funeral for the first apostle of the Northern nations. Theodosius hesitated, and even consented to see the heresiarch Eunomius, who was then living near Constantinople. The Nicenes took alarm, and the Empress Flaccilla urged her husband on the path of persecution. The next edict (Jan. 381) forbade heretical discussions and assemblies inside cities, and ordered the churches everywhere to be given up to the Nicenes.

Suppression of Arian worship inside cities.

Thus was Arianism put down, as it had been set up, by the civil power. Nothing now remained but to clear away the disorders which the strife had left behind. Once more an imperial summons went forth for a council to meet at Constantinople in May 381.

Council of Constantinople (May 381).

It was a sombre gathering. The bright hope which lighted the Empire at Nicæa had long ago died out, and even the conquerors now had no more joyous feeling than that of thankfulness that the weary strife was coming to an end. Only a hundred and fifty bishops were present, all of them Easterns. The West was not represented even by a Roman legate. Amongst them were Meletius of Antioch, Gregory of Nyssa, Cyril of Jerusalem, Gregory of Nazianzus as elect of Constantinople, and Basil's unworthy successor, Helladius of Cæsarea. Timothy of Alexandria came later. The Semiarians mustered thirty-six under Eleusius of Cyzicus.

The bishops were greeted with much splendour, and received a truly imperial welcome in the form of a new edict of persecution against the Manichees.

Appointments of Gregory, Flavian, and Nectarius

Meletius of Antioch presided in the council, and Paulinus was ignored. Theodosius was no longer neutral between Constantinople and Alexandria. The Egyptians were not invited to the earlier sittings, or at least were not present. The first act of the assembly was to ratify the choice of Gregory of Nazianzus as bishop of Constantinople. Meletius died as they were coming to discuss the affairs of Antioch, and Gregory took his place as president. Here was an excellent chance of putting an end to the schism, for Paulinus and Meletius had agreed that on the death of either of them, the survivor should be recognised by both parties as bishop of Antioch. But the council was jealous of Paulinus and his Western friends, and broke the agreement by appointing Flavian, one of the presbyters who had sworn to refuse the office. Gregory's remonstrance against this breach of faith only drew upon him the hatred of the Eastern bishops. The Egyptians, on the other hand, were glad to join any attack on a nominee of Meletius, and found an obsolete Nicene canon to invalidate his translation from Sasima to Constantinople. Both parties were thus agreed for evil. Gregory cared not to dispute with them, but gave up his beloved Anastasia, and retired to end his days at Nazianzus. The council was not worthy of him. His successor was another sort of man. Nectarius, the prætor of Constantinople, was a man of the world of dignified presence, but neither saint nor student. Him, however, Theodosius chose to fill the vacant see, and under his guidance the council finished its sessions.

The next move was to find out whether the Semiarians were willing to share the victory of the Nicenes. Retirement of the Semiarians As they were still a strong party round the Hellespont, their friendship was important. Theodosius also was less of a zealot than some of his admirers imagine. The sincerity of his desire to conciliate Eleusius is fairly guaranteed by his effort two years later to find a scheme of comprehension even for the Anomœans. But the old soldier was not to be tempted by hopes of imperial favour. However he might oppose the Anomœans, he could not forgive the Nicenes their inclusion of the Holy Spirit in the sphere of co-essential deity. Those of the Semiarians who were willing to join the Nicenes had already done so, and the rest were obstinate. They withdrew from the

THE FALL OF ARIANISM. 159

council and gave up their churches like the Arians. They comforted themselves with those words of Scripture, 'The churchmen are many, but the elect are few.'[1]

Whatever jealousies might divide the conquerors, the Arian contest was now at an end. Pontus and Syria were still divided from Rome and Egypt on the question of Flavian's appointment, and there were the germs of many future troubles in the disposition of Alexandria to look for help to Rome against the upstart see of Constantinople; but against Arianism the council was united. Its first canon is a solemn ratification of the Nicene creed in its original shape, with a formal condemnation of all the heresies, 'and specially those of the Eunomians or Anomœans, of the Arians or Eudoxians (*Homœans*), of the Semiarians or Pneumatomachi; of the Sabellians, Marcellians, Photinians, and Apollinarians.'

Close of the council.

The bishops issued no new creed. Tradition indeed ascribes to them the spurious Nicene creed of our Communion Service, with the exception of two later insertions—the clause 'God of God,' and the procession of the Holy Spirit 'from the Son' as well as 'from the Father.' The story is an old one, for it can be traced back to one of the speakers at the council of Chalcedon in 451. It caused some surprise at the time, but was afterwards accepted. Yet it is beyond all question false. This is shown by four convergent lines of argument. In the first place, (1.) it is *a priori* unlikely. The Athanasian party had been contending all along, not vaguely for the Nicene doctrine, but for the Nicene

The spurious Nicene creed

[1] Matt. xx. 16.

creed, the whole Nicene creed, and nothing but the Nicene creed. Athanasius refused to touch it at Sardica in 343, refused again at Alexandria in 362, and to the end of his life refused to admit that it was in any way defective. Basil himself as late as 377 declined even to consider some additions to the incarnation proposed to him by Epiphanius of Salamis. Is it likely that their followers would straightway revise the creed the instant they got the upper hand in 381 ? And such a revision! The elaborate framework of Nicæa is completely shattered, and even the keystone clause 'of the essence of the Father' is left out. Moreover, (2.) there is no contemporary evidence that they did revise it. No historian mentions anything of the sort, and no single document connected with the council gives the slightest colour to the story. There is neither trace nor sign of it for nearly seventy years. The internal evidence (3.) points the same way. Deliberate revision implies a deliberate purpose in the alterations made. Now in this case, though we have serious variations enough, there is another class of differences so meaningless that they cannot even be represented in an English translation. There remains (4.) one more argument. The spurious Nicene creed cannot be the work of the fathers of Constantinople in 381, because it is given in the *Ancoratus* of Epiphanius, which was certainly written in 374. But if the council did not draw up the creed, it is time to ask who did. Everything seems to show that it is not a revision of the Nicene creed at all, but of the local creed of Jerusalem, executed by Bishop Cyril on his return from exile in 362. This is only a theory, but it has all the evidence which a theory can have—it explains the whole matter. In the first place, the meaningless changes disappear if we compare the spurious Nicene creed with that of Jerusalem instead of the genuine Nicene. Every difference can be accounted for by reference to the known position and opinions of Cyril. Thus the old Jerusalem creed says that the Lord '*sat* down at the right hand of the Father;' our 'Nicene,' that he '*sitteth*.' Now this is a favourite point of Cyril in his *Catecheses*—that the Lord did not sit down once for all, but that he sitteth so for ever. Similarly other points. We also know that other local creeds were revised about the same time and in the same way. In the next place, the occurrence of a revised Jerusalem creed in the *Ancoratus* is natural. Epiphanius was past middle life when he left Palestine for Cyprus in 368, and never forgot the friends he left behind at Lydda. We are also in a position to account for its ascription to the council of Constantinople. Cyril's was a troubled life, and there are many indications that he was accused of heresy in 381, and triumphantly acquitted by the council. In such a case his creed would naturally be examined and approved. It was a sound confession, and in no way heretical. From this point its history is clearer. The authority of Jerusalem combined with its own intrinsic merits to recommend it, and the incidental approval of the bishops at Constantinople was gradually developed into the legend of their authorship.

The remaining canons are mostly aimed at the disorders which had grown up during the reign of Valens. One of them checks the reckless accusations which were brought against the bishops by ordering that no charge of heresy should be received from heretics and such like. Such a disqualification of accusers was not unreasonable, as it did not apply to charges of private wrong; yet this clerical privilege grew into one of the worst scandals of the Middle Ages. The forged decretals of the ninth century not only order the strictest scrutiny of witnesses against a bishop, but require seventy-two of them to convict him of any crime *except* heresy. Another canon forbids the intrusion of bishops into other dioceses. 'Nevertheless, the bishop of Constantinople shall hold the first rank after the bishop of Rome, because Constantinople is New Rome.' This is the famous third canon, which laid a foundation for the ecclesiastical authority of Constantinople. It was extended at Chalcedon into a jurisdiction over the whole country from Mount Taurus to the Danube, and by Justinian into the supremacy of the East. The canon, therefore, marks a clear step in the concentration of the Eastern Church and Empire round Constantinople. The blow struck Rome on one side, Alexandria on the other. It was the reason why Rome withheld for centuries her full approval from the council of Constantinople. She could not safely give it till her Eastern rival was humiliated; and this was not till the time of the Latin Emperors in the thirteenth century.

The council having ratified the Emperor's work, it only remained for the Emperor to complete that of the council. A new edict in July forbade Arians of every sort to build churches. Even their old liberty to build

THE FALL OF ARIANISM. 163

outside the walls of cities was now taken from them. At the end of the month Theodosius issued an amended definition of orthodoxy. Henceforth sound belief was to be guaranteed by communion, no longer with Rome and Alexandria, but with Constantinople, Alexandria, and the chief bishoprics of the East. The choice of bishops was decided partly by their own importance, partly by that of their sees. Gregory of Nyssa may represent one class, Helladius of Cæsarea the other. The omissions, however, are significant. We miss not only Antioch and Jerusalem, but Ephesus and Hadrianople, and even Nicomedia. There is a broad space left clear around the Bosphorus If we now take into account the third canon, we cannot mistake the Asiatic policy of endeavouring to replace the primacy of Rome or Alexandria by that of Constantinople

Second edict defining orthodoxy.

The tolerance of Theodosius was a little, though only a little, wider than it seems. Though the Novatians were not in communion with Nectarius, they were during the next half century a recognised exception to the persecuting laws. They had always been sound as against Arianism, and their bishop Agelius had suffered exile under Valens. His confession was approved by Theodosius, and several of his successors lived on friendly terms with liberal or worldly patriarchs like Nectarius and Atticus. They suffered something from the bigotry of Chrysostom, something also from the greed of Cyril, but for them the age of persecution only began with Nestorius in 428.

The Novatians

So far as numbers went, the cause of Arianism was

not even yet hopeless. It was still fairly strong in Syria and Asia, and counted adherents as far west as the banks of the Danube. At Constantinople it could raise dangerous riots (in one of them Nectarius had his house burnt), and even at the court of Milan it had a powerful supporter in Valentinian's widow, the Empress Justina. Yet its fate was none the less a mere question of time. Its cold logic generated no such fiery enthusiasm as sustained the African Donatists; the newness of its origin allowed no venerable traditions to grow up round it like those of heathenism, while its imperial claims and past successes cut it off from the appeal of later heresies to provincial separatism. When, therefore, the last overtures of Theodosius fell through in 383, the heresy was quite unable to bear the strain of steady persecution.

Decay of Arianism.

But if Arianism soon ceased to be a power inside the Empire, it remained the faith of the barbarian invaders. The work of Ulfilas was not in vain. Not the Goths only, but all the earlier Teutonic converts were Arians. And the Goths had a narrow miss of empire. The victories of Theodosius were won by Gothic strength. It was the Goths who scattered the mutineers of Britain, and triumphantly scaled the impregnable walls of Aquileia; the Goths who won the hardest battle of the century, and saw the Franks themselves go down before them on the Frigidus. The Goths of Alaric plundered Rome itself; the Goths of Gainas entered Constantinople, though only to be overwhelmed and slaughtered round the vain asylum of their burning church.

Teutonic Arianism: (1.) In the East.

388.

394

THE FALL OF ARIANISM

In the next century the Teutonic conquest of the West gave Arianism another lease of power. Once more the heresy was supreme in Italy, and Spain, and Africa. Once more it held and lost the future of the world. To the barbarian as well as to the heathen it was a half-way halt upon the road to Christianity; and to the barbarian also it was nothing but a source of weakness. It lived on and in its turn perpetuated the feud between the Roman and the Teuton which caused the destruction of the earlier Teutonic kingdoms in Western Europe. The provincials or their children might forget the wrongs of conquest, but heresy was a standing insult to the Roman world. Theodoric the Ostrogoth may rank with the greatest statesmen of the Empire, yet even Theodoric found his Arianism a fatal disadvantage. And if the isolation of heresy fostered the beginnings of a native literature, it also blighted every hope of future growth. The Goths were not inferior to the English, but there is nothing in Gothic history like the wonderful burst of power which followed the conversion of the English. There is no Gothic writer to compare with Bede or Cædmon. Jordanis is not much to set against them, and even Jordanis was not an Arian.

The sword of Belisarius did but lay open the internal disunion of Italy and Africa. A single blow destroyed the kingdom of the Vandals, and all the valour of the Ostrogoths could only win for theirs a downfall of heroic grandeur. Sooner or later every Arian nation had to purge itself of heresy or vanish from the earth. Even the distant Visigoths were forced to see that Arians could not hold Spain. The Lombards in Italy were the last defenders of the hopeless cause, and they too yielded a few years later to the efforts of Pope Gregory and Queen Theudelinda. Of Continental Teutons, the Franks alone escaped the divisions of Arianism. In the strength of orthodoxy they drove the Goths before them on the field of Vouglé, and brought the green standard of the Prophet to a halt upon the Loire. The Franks were no better than their neighbours—rather worse—so that it was nothing but their orthodoxy which won for them the prize which the Lombard and the Goth had missed, and brought them through a long career of victory to that proud day of universal reconciliation when the strife of ages was forgotten, and Arianism with it—when, after more than three hundred years of desolating anarchy, the Latin and the Teuton joined to vindicate for Old Rome her just inheritance of empire, and to set its holy diadem upon the head of Karl the Frank.

[margin: 599.]
[margin: 507.]
[margin: 732.]
[margin: 800.]

Now that we have traced the history of Arianism to its final overthrow, let us once more glance at the causes of its failure. Arianism, then, was an illogical compromise. It went too far for heathenism, not far enough for Christianity. It conceded Christian worship to the Lord, yet made him no better than a heathen demigod. It confessed a Heavenly Father, as in Christian duty bound, yet identified Him with the mysterious and inaccessible Supreme of the philosophers. As a scheme of Christianity, it was overmatched at every

[margin: Conclusion.]

point by the Nicene doctrine; as a concession to heathenism, it was outbid by the growing worship of saints and relics. Debasing as was the error of turning saints into demigods, it seems to have shocked Christian feeling less than the Arian audacity which degraded the Lord of saints to the level of his creatures But the crowning weakness of Arianism was the incurable badness of its method. Whatever were the errors of Athanasius—and in details they were not a few—his work was without doubt a faithful search for truth by every means attainable to him. He may be misled by his ignorance of Hebrew or by the defective exegesis of his time; but his eyes are always open to the truth, from whatever quarter it may come to him. In breadth of view as well as grasp of doctrine, he is beyond comparison with the rabble of controversialists who cursed or still invoke his name. The gospel was truth and life to him, not a mere subject for strife and debate. It was far otherwise with the Arians. On one side their doctrine was a mass of presumptuous theorizing, supported by alternate scraps of obsolete traditionalism and uncritical text-mongering; on the other it was a lifeless system of spiritual pride and hard unlovingness. Therefore Arianism perished. So too every system, whether of science or theology, must likewise perish which presumes like Arianism to discover in the feeble brain of man a law to circumscribe the revelation of our Father's love in Christ.

CHRONOLOGICAL TABLE.

269. Claudius defeats the Goths at Naissus.
272. Aurelian defeats Zenobia.
284–305 Diocletian.
Cir 297. Birth of Athanasius.
303–313 The great persecution.
306–337 Constantine (in Gaul).
311. First edict of toleration (by Galerius).
312–337. Constantine (in Italy).
312. Second edict of toleration (from Milan).
314 Council of Arles, on the Donatists, &c
315–337. Constantine (in Illyricum).
Cir. 317. Athanasius *de Incarnatione Verbi Dei.*
Cir. 318. Outbreak of Arian controversy.
323–337. Constantine (in the East).
325 (June). Council of Nicæa.
328–373. Athanasius bishop of Alexandria.
330. Foundation of Constantinople.
Cir. 330 Deposition of Eustathius of Antioch.
335. Councils of Tyre and Jerusalem
336 (Feb.)–337 (Nov) First exile of Athanasius.
337 (May 22). Death of Constantine.
339 (Lent)–346 (Oct) Second exile of Athanasius.
341. Council of the Dedication at Antioch. Consecration of Ulfilas.

- 343. Councils of Sardica and Philippopolis.
- 350. Death of Constans.
- 351. Battle of Mursa.
- 353 Death of Magnentius.
- 355. Julian Cæsar in Gaul.
  Council at Milan.
- 356 (Feb 8)–362 (Feb. 22). Third exile of Athanasius.
- 357. Sirmian manifesto.
- 358. Council at Ancyra.
  Hilary *de Synodis*.
- 359 (May 22). Conference at Sirmium. The dated creed.
  Councils of Ariminum and Seleucia.
  Athanasius *de Synodis*.
- 360 (Jan.) Julian Augustus at Paris.
  Council at Constantinople. Exile of Semiarians.
- 361. Appointment and exile of Meletius.
  (Nov.) Death of Constantius.
- 362. Council at Alexandria. Fourth exile of Athanasius.
- 363 (June 26). Death of Julian. Jovian succeeds.
- 364 (Feb. 16). Death of Jovian. Valentinian succeeds.
- 365–366. Revolt of Procopius. Fifth exile and final restoration of Athanasius.
- 367–369 Gothic war.
- 370–379. Basil bishop of Cæsarea (in Cappadocia).
- 371. Death of Marcellus
- 372. Meeting of Basil and Valens.
- 373 (May 2). Death of Athanasius.
- 374. Epiphanius *Ancoratus*.
- 374–397. Ambrose bishop of Milan.
- 375. Death of Valentinian. Gratian succeeds.
- 376. Goths pass the Danube.
- 378 (Aug. 9). Battle of Hadrianople. Death of Valens.
- 379–395. Theodosius Emperor.
- 381 (May.) Council of Constantinople.

383. Last overtures of Theodosius to the Arians.
397. Chrysostom bishop of Constantinople.
410. Sack of Rome by Alaric.
451. Council of Chalcedon.
487–526. Reign of Theodoric in Italy.
507 Battle of Vouglé.
589. Visigoths abandon Arianism.
599. Lombards abandon Arianism.
800. Coronation of Karl the Frank.

THE FAMILY OF CONSTANTINE

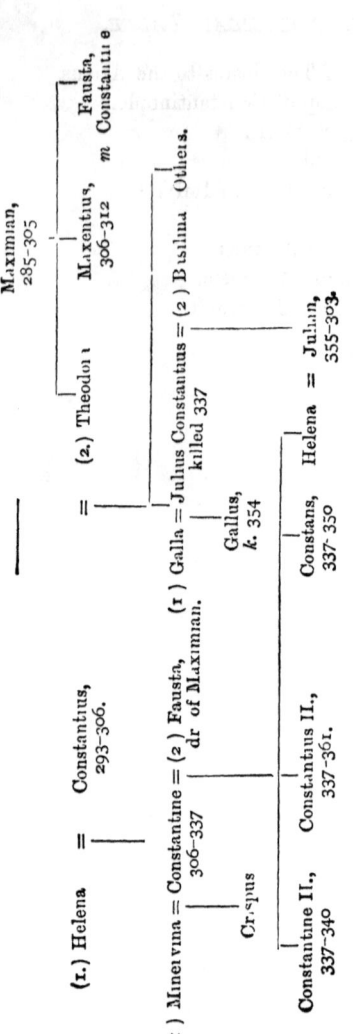

INDEX.

ACACIUS, Bishop of Cæsarea, 42, 49; at Sardica, 70, 90, forms Homœan party, 92, at Seleucia, 97; character, 100, at Constantinople, 101, and Meletius, 103, 104, accepts Nicene faith, 115, 120, 124

Aetius, Anomœan doctrine, 75, ordained by Leontius, 78, 100, degraded, 101.

Agelius, Novatian bishop of Constantinople, 163

Alaric, 164

Alexander, Bishop of Alexandria, 5; excommunicates Arius, 14, 19, at Nicæa, 21, death of, 47, and Athanasius, 48

Alexander, Bishop of Thessalonica, at Tyre, 57, 58

Ambrose, Bishop of Milan, 122, 134; Illyrian council, 146, 151.

Ammianus, historian, 109.

Anastasia church, 153

Anthimus, Bishop of Tyana, quarrels with Basil, 135, 153, with Gregory of Nyssa, 145

Antony, legendary hermit, 48, 123

Apollinarius of Laodicea, 12, 113, 124; doctrine, 136-142, 145.

Arinthæus the Goth, 132.

Arius, early life and doctrine, 5; excommunicated, 14, flees to Cæsarea, 15, 19, exiled, 38, restored at Jerusalem, 58, death, 59, 68, 75, 77, and Apollinarius, 137

Ascholius, Bishop of Thessalonica, baptizes Theodosius, 155.

Asterius, Cappadocian sophist, 131.

Athanaric, Goth, 148, death, 155.

Athanasius, *de Incarnatione*, 9-12; as a commentator, 13, 49, 167, at Nicæa, 21, persistence, 27, account of Nicene debates, 34, dislikes Meletian settlement, 38, policy at Nicæa, 39, 46, 47, Bishop of Alexandria, 48, character and early life, 48, power in Egypt, 50, 87, 114, 122; at Tyre, 57, flees to Constantinople, 58, 87, first exile, 59, return, 62, second exile, 64, 68, at Sardica, 70, second return, 73, overtures of Magnentius, 81, expelled by Syrianus, 86, third exile, 87, on Homœan reasoning, 94, *de Synodis*, 97, 98, third return, 111, at council of Alexandria, 112, fourth exile, 114, fourth return, 120, 122, on the Holy Spirit, 125, troubles with Valens, 127, final restoration, 129, and Basil, 132, 134, and Apollinarius, 137-141, last years, reception of Marcellus, 142, death, 143, 151, holds to Nicene creed, 160

Aurelian, Emperor (270-275), services, 16, test of Christian orthodoxy, 24

Auxentius, Arian bishop of Milan, 102, 121, Cappadocian, 131.

BAPTISMAL professions, 23

Basil, Bishop of Ancyra, expelled, 62; restored, 82, at synod of Ancyra, 90, 132, 98, returns, 111

Basil, Bishop of Cæsarea (Cappadocia), 109, on the Holy Spirit, 125, life and work, 132-136, on reception of Marcellians, 144, 145, death, 151, student life, 152; holds to Nicene creed, 160

Basilina, mother of Julian, 105, 106

Belisarius, 165

CÆCILIAN, Bishop of Carthage, at Nicæa, 20.

Cappadocia, 130

Carpones, an early Arian, 14, at Rome, 65

Chrysostom (John), 43, 46, 163

Claudius, Bishop in Picenum, 100

Constans, Emperor (337-350), 62, 69, 73, death, 80

Constantia, sister of Constantine, 25

Constantine, Emperor (306–337), character, 17; dealings with Arianism, 18, summons Nicene council, 19, action there, 36, 37, 47, church on Golgotha, 57, 76; exiles Athanasius, 59; work and death, 61, church at Antioch, 67, 87, power of his name, 80, 127, 128, 148

Constantine II, Emperor (337–340), 62, death, 70

Constantius, Emperor (337–361), 45 46; accession and character, 62; calls Sardican council, 70, recalls Athanasius, 73; defeats Magnentius, 81; pressure on the West, 82, exiles Liberius, 85, expels Athanasius, 86, 101, 103, death of, 106, 112

Councils
Alexandria (362), 112.
Ancyra (358), 90.
Antioch (269), 33
  „   (338), 64.
  „   (341), 67.
  „   (344), 72
Ariminum (359), 93.
Arles (314), 20
  „   (353), 70
Constantinople (360), 101
  „   (381), 157.
Lampsacus (364), 125.
Jerusalem (335), 58.
Milan (355), 83
Nicæa (325), 19–40.
Sardica (343), 70.
Seleucia (359), 93.
Tyre (335), 57.

Creeds
Antioch (first), 68.
  „   (second = Lucianic), 68
  „   (third = Tyana), 69.
  „   (fourth), 69.
  „   (fifth), 72
Apostles' (Marcellus), 22, 67
Cæsarea, 26.
Constantinople (360), 101
"Constantinople" (381), 159
Jerusalem, 77, 159
Nicæa (genuine), 29
  „   (spurious), 159.
Nicé, 95
Sardica (Philippopolis), 72.
Seleucia, 97
Sirmium (manifesto), 88
  „   (dated), 94

Cyril, Bishop of Alexandria, 163
Cyril, Bishop of Jerusalem, *Catecheses*, 76; accepts Nicene faith, 115, 147, 151; at Constantinople, 157, and "Nicene" creed, 160, 161

DALMATIUS, 62
Damasus, Bishop of Rome, 155.

Demophilus, Bishop of Constantinople, 122, 145, 151, gives up the churches, 156
Dianius, Bishop of Cæsarea (Cappadocia), 115; baptizes Basil, 132.
Diocletian, Emperor (284–305), persecution, 9; reign, 17
Diodorus, Bishop of Tarsus, 78
Dionysius, Bishop of Milan, exiled, 82, 83, 90.
Dominica, Empress, 126.
Donatists, 18, 20
Dorotheus, Arian bishop of Antioch, 151

ELEUSIUS, Bishop of Cyzicus, at Seleucia, 96, 97, 115, at Lampsacus, 125; at Constantinople, 157, 158
Epiphanius, Bishop of Salamis, 160, 161
Eudoxius, Bishop of Constantinople, 75; Bishop of Antioch, 90, 97; translated to Constantinople, 102; 104, 115, 120; 122, deposed at Lampsacus, 125, influence with Valens, 126, 129, Cappadocian, 131, 145
Eugenius, deacon, 142.
Euippius, Arian bishop, 132, 133
Eunomius, Anomœan, 75, 95, Bishop of Cyzicus, 103, 115, on the Holy Spirit, 125, exiled, 130, Cappadocian, 131; 156
Euphrates, Bishop of Cologne, 72.
Euphronius, Bishop of Antioch, 51.
Eusebia, Empress, 105
Eusebius, Bishop of Cæsarea (Palestine), countenances Arius, 15, 21, action at Nicæa, 25; proposes Cæsarean creed, 35, signs Nicene, 36; 42; caution after Nicæa, 47; 49, 51, at Tyre, 57, 58, succeeded by Acacius, 70, 100
Eusebius, Bishop of Cæsarea (Cappadocia), 132
Eusebius, Bishop of Nicomedia, favours Arius, 15; at Nicæa, 21, presents Arianizing creed, 25, 37, exiled, 38, organizes new party, 50; attacks Athanasius, 56, 59
Eusebius, Bishop of Samosata, 133, 151; murder of, 152
Eusebius, Bishop of Vercellæ, exiled, 83, 90, restored, 111, at Alexandria, 112
Eustathius, Bishop of Antioch, at Nicæa, 21, 34, exiled, 51, and Apollinarius, 137
Eustathius, Bishop of Sebastia, at Ancyra, 91, 103, at Lampsacus, 126; exiled by Valens, goes to Liberius, 128, 132, quarrels with Basil, 135, 136, 145
Euzoius, an early Arian, 14, 58, 68;

INDEX.

Bishop of Antioch, 104, 115, 120, 124; death, 151.

FLAVIAN, Bishop of Antioch, 78, 158.
Flavianus, prefect of Egypt, 127
Fortunatian, Bishop of Aquileia, 70.
Fritigern, Goth, 148, death, 154

GAINAS, 164.
Galatia, 52
Gallus, Cæsar, 62, 105.
George of Cappadocia, Arian bishop of Alexandria, 86, 87; deposed at Seleucia, 97, and Julian, 107, lynched, 111, 112, 131
Germinius, Bishop of Cyzicus, translated to Sirmium, 82.
Gothic wars, first, 129; second (Hadrianople), 149-155
Gratian, Emperor (375-383), 149, edict of toleration, 151, takes Theodosius for colleague, 154.
Gratus of Carthage, 70
Gregory of Nazianzus, consecrates Basil, 133, 152
Gregory of Nazianzus (son of the above), 151, life and work at Constantinople, 152, 156; Bishop of Constantinople, 157, 158
Gregory, Bishop of Nyssa, 141, 145, at Constantinople, 157, 163
Gregory, Bishop of Rome, 166.
Gregory of Cappadocia; Arian bishop of Alexandria, 64; death of, 73, 86, 131
Gregory the Wonder-worker, 132.

HANNIBALIANUS, 62
Hecebolius, renegade, 107
Helladius, Bishop of Cæsarea (Cappadocia), 157, 163
Hilarion, legendary hermit, 123.
Hilary, Bishop of Poitiers, 46, 67, 82, exile and character, 84, 90, denounces Liberius, 92, his *de Synodis*, 93; at Seleucia, 96, 112; on the Holy Spirit, 124
Hosius, Bishop of Cordova, at Nicæa, 20, 34, 37, at Sardica, 70, 72, 82, exile and death, 85, 90.

JAMES, Bishop of Nisibis, at Nicæa, 21
Jerusalem in 348, 76
John Archaph, Meletian, exiled, 59
John the Persian at Nicæa, 22
Jordanis, 165
Jovian, Emperor (363-364), 119, 120.
Julian, Emperor (361-363), 40, 43, 46, 47, 62, made Cæsar, 83, Augustus, 102; his reign, 105-117, ascetic leanings, 108, 123, education edict, 109, 137, exiles Athanasius, 114, 127, results,

118, 122; and Cappadocia, 130; student life, 152
Julius, Bishop of Rome, receives Athanasius and Marcellus, 65; 70, 72, 85, 88
Julius Constantius, 105.
Justina, Empress, 164.

KARL the Great, coronation of, 166.

LACTANTIUS on the persecutors, 11.
Leonas, 97
Leontius, Bishop of Antioch, appointed, 72, management, 78, 104
Libanius, heathen rhetorician, 43; friend of Basil, 132
Liberius, Bishop of Rome, 82, disavows Vincent, 83, exile of, 85, 90; signs Sirmian creed, 91, receives Semiarian deputation, 128
Licinius, Emperor (306-323), 15, 19
Lucian of Antioch, teacher of Arius, 5; of Eusebius of Nicomedia, 15, disciples at Nicæa, 21, left no successors, 46, disciples after Nicæa, 50, connection with Aetius, 75
Lucianic creed, at Antioch, 68; 77, 91; at Seleucia, 97, 115; at Lampsacus, 126
Lucifer, Bishop of Calaris, exile and writings, 83, 90, returns, 111, absent from Alexandria, 112; consecrates Paulinus, 114, forms schism, 124, 134
Lucius, Arian bishop of Alexandria, 142, 144, 147

MACARIUS, Bishop of Ælia (Jerusalem), 15, at Nicæa, 21
Macedonius, Bishop of Constantinople, 79, 115
Magnentius, Emperor (350-353), 74; 80, 82
Marcellus, Bishop of Ancyra, at Nicæa, 21, and Apostles' creed, 23, 67, persistence, 27, 31, 32, and Nicene creed, 47, 51, character and doctrine, 52-56, exiled, 59, restored, 62, flees to Rome, 65, at Sardica, 70, 72, attacked by Cyril, 77, deposed, 81; 90, 103, returns, 111, embassy to Athanasius, 142, death, 143, extinction of his school, 144
Mardonius, 105, 107
Maris, Bishop of Chalcedon, at Nicæa, 21, curses Julian, 111, 117
Maximin (Daza), Emperor (305-313), 48
Maximus, Bishop of Jerusalem, 57, 58; receives Athanasius, 73
Maximus, Bishop of Trier, 70
Meletius, Bishop of Antioch, 78, trans

lated from Sebastia, 1034 exiled, 104; return, 113, 115, accepts Nicene creed, 120, exiled by Valens, 128, restored, 129, 131, 134, 147, 151, death at Constantinople, 157
Meletus, Bishop of Lycopolis, 19, Nicene settlement, 38
Modestus, renegade, 132, 133.

NECTARIUS, Bishop of Constantinople, 158, 163, 164
Nepotianus, Emperor (350), 80.
Nestorius, Bishop of Constantinople, 163.

ORIGEN, 9, 33, 76, 113; on the Holy Spirit, 124

PAPHNUTIUS, confessor, at Nicæa, 21; at Tyre, 57, 58
Paul, Bishop of Neocæsarea, at Nicæa, 21
Paul of Samosata, 33, 91
Paul of Thebes, legendary hermit, 123
Paulinus, 51, consecrated by Lucifer, 114, 147, ignored at Constantinople, 157, 158
Paulinus, Bishop of Trier, 82, 83, 90
Pegasius, Bishop of Ilium, apostate, 108
Pelagius, Bishop of Laodicea, 104
Peter, Bishop of Alexandria, 144, 152, 155
Philagrius, expels Athanasius, 64, 86
Phœbadius, Bishop of Agen, condemns Sirmian manifesto, 90, at Ariminum, 99, 101
Photinus, Bishop of Sirmium, condemned, 73, deposed, 81, 90, 91
Pistus, an early Arian, 14, Arian bishop of Alexandria, 64, 65
Pœmenius, Anomœan bishop of Constantinople, 120
Potammon, confessor, at Nicæa, 21, at Tyre, 57, 58
Proæresius, teacher of Julian, 109, 152.
Procopius, revolt of, 128
Protasius, Bishop of Milan, 70

RESTACES, Armenian bishop at Nicæa, 22

SABELLIANISM, its meaning, 9; relation of Athanasius to, 12, 32, general dislike of, 13, relation of Marcellus to, 32
Sasima, 153
Sebastian the Manichee, outrages in Egypt, 86, commands against Goths 149
Secundus, Bishop of Ptolemais, at Nicæa, 21, refuses Nicene creed, 38, consecrates Pistus, 64, 65.
Serapion, Bishop of Thmuis, 125.
Silvanus the Frank, 81
Silvanus, Bishop of Tarsus, at Seleucia, 95, 97
Socrates, historian, 79
Stephen, Bishop of Antioch, at Sardica, 70, deposed, 72
Syrianus, *dux Ægypti*, expels Athanasius, 86.

TERTULLIAN, 9.
Theodoric, 165
Theodosius, Emperor (379-395), choice of and character, 154, first rescript, 155; calls council of Constantinople, 157, second rescript, 163
Theodotus, Bishop of Nicopolis, 136
Theonas, Bishop of Marmarica, at Nicæa, 21, refuses Nicene creed, 38.
Theophilus the Goth, at Nicæa, 22.
Theophilus the Indian, 120.
Theophronius, Bishop of Tyana, 69.
Theudelinda, Lombard queen, 166
Timothy, Bishop of Alexandria, 157

ULFILAS, death, 156, 164
Ursacius, Bishop of Singidunum, and Sirmian manifesto, 88, 90, 91, forms Homœan party, 92, at Ariminum, 95.

VALENS, Emperor (364-378), 46, character, 121, church and state under, 122, 144, 161, 124, Homœan policy, 126, fresh exiles, 127, Procopian panic, 128, baptism and first Gothic war, 129, overawed by Basil, 133, second Gothic war, 149, death at Hadrianople, 150
Valens, Bishop of Mursa, and Sirmian manifesto, 88, 90, 91, forms Homœan party, 92, at Ariminum, 95, 99, 101, 130
Valentinian, Emperor (364-375), character and policy, 121, Semiarian deputation to, 128, 131, death, 146
Vetranio, Emperor (350), 80, 81.
Victor, a Sarmatian, 132
Victorinus, Marius, 109
Vincent, Bishop of Capua, at Nicæa, 20, at Sardica, 70, at Antioch, 72, yields at Arles, 83
Vitalis, Apollinarian bishop of Antioch, 141.

www.ingramcontent.com/pod-product-compliance
Lightning Source LLC
Chambersburg PA
CBHW071424160426
43195CB00013B/1800